UNDERSTANDING OUR CULTURE

An Anthropological View

UNDERSTANDING OUR CULTURE
An Anthropological View

Wendell H. Oswalt
University of California, Los Angeles

HOLT, RINEHART AND WINSTON, INC.
New York   Chicago   San Francisco   Atlanta   Dallas
Montreal   Toronto   London   Sydney

N 106

To my children—Bill, Pam, Ivar

PREFACE

Anthropology has been nurtured on the study of nonliterate peoples, living or dead, and on their achievements. The traditional interests of anthropologists lead them to an involvement with fossilized human bones and ancient tools of stone as well as with living peoples who can neither read nor write. However, as most broadly conceived, anthropology is above all else a point of view and a set of concepts for understanding the nature of all men and their shared behavioral ways. Yet it is the sociologist who speaks most authoritatively about modern complex societies, the political scientist and the economist who deal with even narrower topics within the confines of Western culture, and the historian who reconstructs man's past from the writings of diverse persons. In its broadest context, anthropology includes all the subject matter just mentioned, but, in reality, it has only recently begun to concentrate on modern men in complex societies.

By and large anthropologists find satisfaction in their intellectual niche, for they have built an empirically snug, if theoretically tenuous, nest for themselves; yet some anthropologists have uncomfortable feelings about their empirical base. The discomfort is particularly apparent among ethnographers, whose work is the vital heart of anthropology. Ethnographers traditionally have studied exotic peoples who are called tribal, nonliterate, primitive, or less often, savage or barbarian. Knowledge about these strangers has been obtained in part by participation in their normal and special activities, and the information has been recorded in elaborate detail. But lo the poor ethnographer of today. Except in the wilds of highland New Guinea and in some jungle recesses of South America there are no pristine primitives who have remained beyond the call of missionaries, traders, and travelers. Given the zeal of some persons to save souls, the hopes of others for economic gain, and the range of tourist jets, the ethnographer today must nearly always compromise his ideals. He may settle among once-primitive peoples whose old customs are fading away. He often shares their sadness and frustrations as he methodically records a way of life being consumed by the Western world. Many ethnographers have become disenchanted with describing the impending doom of tribal peoples, for they find that there is often a bland sameness to the paths their subjects follow toward the Western world. Furthermore, there is a sense of futility in plotting the ways of dying peoples without being able to stem the disease with which they are afflicted.

Other anthropologists have turned away from the primitives so dear to the hearts of most of their colleagues but for different reasons. They are concerned, perplexed, and even angered by the direction in which they see the modern world moving. Such individuals turn their backs on nonliterate peoples in the hope of being able to better use their knowledge to influence the present and to help insure the future, whereas their past-oriented colleagues deny the competence of anthropology to deal with the complexities of the modern world. The now-and-tomorrow-directed anthropologists argue that if any one group of trained researchers should be able to cast modern America, or even the modern world, into a meaningful framework it is those whose legitimate focus is on all of mankind. No other group of scientists has a perspective comparable to that of the anthropologist from which to view the diversity in human ways. We have an ongoing curiosity and a breadth of knowledge about man that is unparalleled. We should be in a better position than anyone else to interpret man's social and cultural behavior, and even our mistakes probably are more reasonable and more logical than those of many other observers. With this attitude some of us emerge as secular crusaders searching for a contemporary message. Unquestionably, we sometimes ask irrelevant questions and arrive at answers which in the near future might illustrate our ignorance much more than our learning. Anthropology is youthful, and anthropologists do not pretend to be seers or to offer panaceas. We accept the challenge of understanding man's existence, but we must grope uncomfortably in our efforts to provide insight into what is happening among modern peoples.

This, as all books, is addressed to a particular readership. I hope to reach persons who are unaware of the aims of anthropologists as well as those who think that anthropologists deal only in arrowheads, human bones, or bizarre stories about naked peoples. My primary purpose is to discuss present-day man in the United States and to explain how we came to be what we are, both within an anthropological framework. My secondary aim is to encourage thoughts about our future, after first seeing ourselves within a cross-cultural view. This book is designed primarily as a college and university text. It should be appropriate as the primary text in courses about the United States in most academic departments. Perhaps it is best suited for those courses which focus on ourselves in anthropology and sociology departments. It also is hoped that instructors in introductory courses in sociocultural anthropology will find this book useful as a supplement to their major text. Such usage might convey to students that anthropologists do have a concern with our own as well as tribal peoples.

I must note that after consulting items cited in the

bibliography I have strayed from and even contra-
dicted the conclusions of some authors, but I have not
attempted to justify my differences. They are presented as my own, however, and must stand or fall
on that basis.

W. H. O.

Los Angeles, California
November 1969

ACKNOWLEDGMENTS

Professor George D. Spindler read two drafts of this manuscript, and his highly perceptive suggestions were incorporated into the final copy. I gratefully acknowledge his invaluable service. Mrs. Barbara Collins diligently sought out many of the sources utilized, and I am pleased to express my sincere thanks to her for devotion to the task. My wife, Helen Taylor Oswalt, edited each draft of the manuscript and served as a severe but always constructive critic. To her my debt is greatest and my thanks abundant.

CONTENTS

1

POINTS OF VIEW

In moments of exuberance I feel that anthropology is all things to all men, but more somber reflections lead me to rephrase my assessment in more realistic terms. Anthropology admittedly is nothing to many people; it is an obscure topic to others; but to some it offers a point of view about man. As normally conceived in educational terms, anthropology is an academic discipline within the social or behavioral sciences, but a label such as this cannot begin to convey the place of anthropology in the world of man today. Because it offers a studied perspective for viewing ourselves and all other peoples, living or dead, anthropology has profound implications for all men. Furthermore, it provides a framework for studying all that men have accomplished and will accomplish in the future. Each of the other sciences, whether it is precise like physics or less exact like sociology, lacks the breadth and the vitality conveyed in the very simple statement: "We study man." It is a self-evident truth that in the absence of man we are nothing, and therefore it is imperative for us to know ourselves and other peoples who are either similar or dissimilar. Anthropology is a great intellectual as well as a very practical challenge arising out of man's presence; it exists and expands because a group of individuals has accepted the obligation of studying man's past, present, and future in a broad perspective. Almost as many orientations are present in anthropology as there are anthropologists, for a tightly conceived intellectual framework in which to order the data and theories is yet to be developed. In spite of this basic inadequacy anthropologists are able to isolate concepts which reveal a great deal about people and their behavior. I consider it a privilege to be able to present certain critical ideas which lead to a better understanding of the reality of man.

PATTERNS AND BEHAVIOR To single out a particular concept and label it as the most basic of empirical truths would be presumptive, and yet in a search for fundamentals one principle stands out. It is that there is order and coherence in all aspects of life. This is true of human behavior as it relates to ideas, other persons, man-made things, and the natural world. Human actions are built of bits and pieces giving rise to plans or models which are called patterns. Patterns emerge through the unification of behavioral particulars and exist both in the natural and man-made worlds. Patterns in nature are to be seen, for example, in the arrangement of leaves on a tree, in the composition of a tree's bark, or in the location of one tree with reference to another. Patterns in human biology include the symmetry of our limb arrangement and the particular composition of our blood. Biological patterns, including those in man, are of less concern in the present context than are those patterns knowingly and unknowingly created by men. Thus, our focus will be on man's creations, whether they are particular ways of behaving such as tipping one's hat and thumbing one's nose or types of manufactures such as ice cream or jet aircraft.

A pattern is an arrangement of components into a system, and the resultant systems may be conceived of as existing at varying levels of abstraction. In the broadest and most obtuse realm are the *universal patterns*, or gross, abstract categories of behavior shared by all peoples. Included among the universal patterns are language, knowledge, social and political norms, supernatural beliefs, manufactures, and the arts. These generalized patterns are found among all peoples, but each population segment exhibits its own unique configuration of particulars. The distinctive combination of ways to which a particular people adheres gives rise to its *tribal* or *national pattern*. At a more specific level are the *systemic patterns*, each of which is a component of the national pattern. Systemic patterns in turn are composed of *particular patterns*, and these are built of bits and pieces called *elements* or *traits*.

The levels of pattern, from those forms composed of the smallest elements to those of universal applicability, provide a rather simple means for classifying social and cultural behavior from its very specific to its most general forms. Thus, in terms of the universal pattern in language, our national pattern is English, whereas that of other nations may be French, Russian, Spanish, or a host of other languages. We have particular social norms, such as a stress on the small or nuclear family consisting of a man, his wife, and their children, which combine to form our national pattern for this universal. Other peoples may emphasize different familial units as the basis for their social life, and this would be a part of their national pattern of social norms. Regardless of which pattern develops, all peoples must address themselves to social matters, just as all must in some way deal with supernaturals, the manufacture of material objects, or any of the other universals; universal patterns are the common denominators of the ways of life shared by men everywhere. At the level of national patterns, our dialects of English are unique to us, our knowledge is not quite the same in its configuration as that found anywhere else in the world, our political institutions are distinctive, and so on through the range of universals; it is these distinctive patterns which give the United States its unique national stamp. In terms of our systemic patterns, we may note one which might be labeled transportation. Within this system our freeways, highways, and streets form a particular pattern as modifications of the natural environment. We also see around us a different but particular pattern in the existence of vehicles, including automobiles, trucks, and motorcycles. Another particular pattern covers the social and political aspects, including the functions of policemen and laws relevant to transportation. At all levels, from the very specific to the very abstract, both in the world of nature and of man, there is order or pattern, and the description of these patternings should provide a basic guide for understanding man and mankind's diversities.

A PATTERN ELEMENT: AMERICAN BUTTONS   In order to illustrate the pattern concept and its significance more fully, it is worthwhile to discuss one form of manufactured item in detail. The example selected is the metal buttons made in the United States between 1700 and 1812. These buttons represent an element or trait within our historic and particular pattern of clothing. A glance around the world indicates a great variability in fastenings which serve the same purpose as buttons; they include the toggle bars used among Eskimos, loops sewn on Chinese garments, and tie strings which have been popular in many places. In the West, however, it is buttons which are the old and well-established form of fastening on garments. Considering the wear and tear to which fastenings are subjected, we would expect considerable experimentation in the production of buttons. The assumption is that any technological manufacture can be improved, and this clearly includes buttons.

For the sake of brevity I will deal only with the plain, relatively flat, metal buttons with eyes at the back which were made in the United States during a little more than one hundred years. Between 1700 and 1765 such buttons were generally made of brass or bronze. During that period the button and its wedge-shaped shank were cast as one piece, and a hole was drilled through the shank for the insertion of thread (Figure 1a). A button of this type—a type being an abstrac-

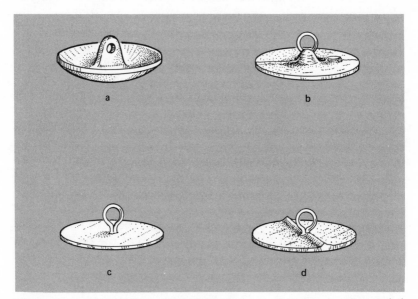

a   b

c   d

Figure 1. *American buttons, 1700–1812 (Courtesy of Stanley J. Olsen and the Society for American Archaeology).*

tion which represents a group—had a number of obvious disadvantages, one of which was that the thin shank might break loose. A greater disadvantage probably was that these buttons often were lost because the thread parted after rubbing against the rough edges of the drilled eye hole. Thus, this was not a perfect button by any means, but it already was a rather complex form. Between 1760 and 1790 another type of button was produced. It was cast from white metal, which is made from a lead or tin base, and had a central mold seam; a wire eye of iron was fitted into a raised section at the center of the back (Figure 1b). The wire would not abrade thread as quickly as did the previous shank, but if it pulled free from the cast metal, broke, or wore away, the button became useless. From 1785 to 1800, and probably somewhat later, most buttons were made of brass or bronze; more importantly, the eye was soldered to the cast button (Figure 1c). The problem most often encountered was that the eye pulled loose; eyeless buttons of this type often have been found in archeological excavations. Beginning in 1812, brass wire was used to make eyes that had short, right-angle projections or feet at the base; these were soldered to the brass or bronze buttons (Figure 1d). The projections at the base made the eye much less likely to pull free, and thus an attachment problem for a particular type of metal button was solved after more than a hundred years of use and experimentation.

Although it is impossible to prove why most of the button types failed, the assumptions are quite logical in terms of button problems to this day. These button types illustrate the nature of change in a particular trait during four consecutive periods in time. Throughout the alterations each type retains a congruity and logic in its configurational whole. No button is two feet across; none is cast of wax or has a microscopic eye. These and other possibilities are incongruous with the accepted norms in button design. The changes which have been made in the type of eye, the metal used, and the method of casting all are attempts to perfect a form. Although each particular button type is distinctive, it is possible to visualize continuity in the development of one form from another; each type logically as well as historically emerged from an earlier form. When we begin at one point in time, 1700 in this case, and determine the modifications in an element through an extended period, we see the dynamic aspect of such modifications within a particular pattern. In this example, a developmental or cumulative type of technological change emerges. A cumulative change, at any level of abstraction, reflects ordered and logical modifications which may be theoretically extended to become predictive models.

As manufactured objects, these buttons have physical form which may be measured, weighed, and described. In terms of these formal components, a button comprises a *structure*. When it is thought of in terms of purpose, we are concerned with its *function*, the end it serves which justifies the structure. Buttons function as a means of garment attachment. Thus, structure and function are closely related concepts of the same pertinence as morphology and physiology in organisms. In the concepts of structure and function, however, there is no implicit allowance for changes over time. Each of the four button forms considered alone is a separate, discrete, and static structure. When we begin to analyze changes and to note the relatedness from one form to the next, the dimension of time becomes critical. The concept of *process,* meaning the consideration of structure and function over time, provides the necessary dimension to examine why one form of button changed into another but related form. Thus, all structures are composed of formal units which have specific functions, and when they change, we observe process. It is in terms of these particular concepts that all patterns arise, linger, and pass into other patterns.

A PARTICULAR PATTERN: SANTA CLAUS   The button example illustrated the changes in an element, a type of garment attachment, within a particular pattern—United States clothing styles. Buttons are physical objects with precise and visible form. On the other hand, the pattern quality also exists in elements which are manifest largely in thoughts and are only secondarily given tangible form. An imaginary but nonetheless particular form of pattern is that represented by Santa Claus, who, like all new creations, developed from certain elements of previously existing patterns being combined and modified to produce a novel form.

The most likely lineal ancestor of Santa Claus is Saint Nicholas, a bishop of Myra in Lycia, Asia Minor, who possibly died in the year A.D. 345 and was canonized in the ninth century. Although little is recorded about his life, he is known as a patron of such diverse groups as sailors, thieves, and most importantly, children. Eventually St. Nicholas became the patron saint of the Dutch maritime center of Amsterdam, with its complement of sailors and navigators, whom he reportedly favored. A church was dedicated to St. Nicholas in Amsterdam, and as the city prospered, he was given partial credit for its success. His Feast Day, December 6, was commemorated with the distribution of candies, cakes, and cookies. The rise of Protestantism in the Netherlands led some clergymen to oppose the traditional recognition of St. Nicholas because of his associations with the Roman Catholic Church; however, St. Nicholas' Day continued to be commemorated. It appears that in the Netherlands a second figure, Woden, who was even more remote than St. Nicholas, also was associated with the month of December. He traveled on a white horse, wore a magic cloak, and dispensed gifts to children; it was customary for hopeful children to set out something for his horse to eat. Parts of these two concepts were merged, and the resultant St. Nicholas arrived annually on the night of December 5th. He rode a white horse and wore the red robes of a bishop. On this evening children placed their shoes and hay for the saint's horse near the fireplace. St. Nicholas arrived on the rooftop of a house, descended through the chimney, and placed candy and cookies in the shoes of good children but left birch rods for bad children.

In pre-Santa Claus times diverse supernatural gift-givers, of whom St. Nicholas was probably the most important, existed in European countries. Among Western Slavs and Germanic peoples in general St. Nicholas gave presents to children on the eve of December 6th, but in Spain the Three Kings were the bearers of gifts, which were given on Twelfth Night, the day of the Epiphany. In Italy gifts were dropped down the chimney on Twelfth Night by a kindly witch, Befana. Although each of these gift-givers arrived during the Christmas season, none has more than a remote relationship to Santa Claus.

Our concept of Santa Claus, the folk hero, clearly appears to be a direct outgrowth of the religious figure St. Nicholas as he existed in the beliefs of the Dutch settlers of New York. In the early years of the nineteenth century the New York Dutch conceived of St. Nicholas as vaulting through the sky from one rooftop to another in a horse-drawn wagon. He descended chimneys bearing gifts for good children and switches for those who were bad. In preparation for his arrival, children put hay beside the fireplace to feed his horses, and they hung their stockings by the fireplace so that St. Nicholas might fill them with gifts. During this period he apparently arrived either on the eve of December 6th or on Christmas Eve, and he might be called St. Nicholas or Santa Claus; the latter term is a modification of the word Sinterklaus, a Dutch alternative for Sint Nikolaas. Between 1812 and 1822, Santa Claus as we know him today began to emerge with greater clarity. Washington Irving in his 1812 edition of *A History of New York . . . by Diedrich Knickerbocker* mentions that St. Nicholas rode in a wagon. A poem published on December 1, 1815, in a New York newspaper asks Sancte Claus or St. Nicholas to bring gifts for children's stockings and states that if he forgets anything, "Let that be the Rod." A second poem memorable in the history of Santa Claus was published in 1821 by a New York resident named William B. Gilley and titled "The Children's Friend." In this poem and in the accompanying illustration, Santa arrives in a sled drawn by a reindeer for the first time (Figure 2). A third poem, this one written by Clement C. Moore in 1822, to entertain his family, combined the meter of the 1815 newspaper poem with a meaning similar to that of the Gilley poem. Moore's poem was copied by a relative and appeared in a newspaper the following year under the title "An Account of a Visit from

Figure 2. *The earliest illustration of Santa Claus arriving in a reindeer-drawn sled (Courtesy of American Antiquarian Society).*

St. Nicholas"; it has come to be known also as " 'Twas the Night Before Christmas," which are the first words of the poem. Moore did not acknowledge his authorship until the poem appeared in a book of poetry published in 1837. The text of Moore's poem is so well known that it hardly requires summary, but it may be noted that it was he who introduced the "eight tiny rein-deer." In spite of the now-familiar ideas about Santa Claus which were beginning to emerge, he was still portrayed as a Dutch saint. A painting of St. Nicholas made in 1837 by Robert W. Weir was inspired by Moore's poem but shows a Dutch saint complete with his emblem, a pipe, Dutch boots, and a rosary. It was not until the early 1860s that our folk hero known as Santa Claus completely assumed his traditional American form. The person most responsible for the transition was Thomas Nast (1840–1902), the first American political cartoonist. Beginning in 1863 his illustrations of Santa Claus appeared nearly every year until 1886. It was Nast who made Santa into a large, jolly, fur-clad, bearded bringer of gifts in the stereotypic form that we accept to this day (Figure 3). The emergence

Figure 3. The earliest illustration of Santa Claus in modern form (Courtesy of the Bettmann Archive Inc.).

of our distinctive Santa Claus during this era, particularly if, as it seems, he became himself between about 1820 and 1865, is quite in keeping with other developments in our cultural history. It was during this span of time, especially between 1840 and 1860, that we were purposefully as well as unknowingly creating our own distinct form of national culture. Between the panics of 1837 and 1857 there was great prosperity, our population almost doubled, and we were becoming quite sure of ourselves as a nation. It is no accident, for example, that the first great American songwriter, Stephen Foster (1826–1864), gained acceptance during this time.

Santa Claus was an American myth and may have been created to counteract the harsh materialism of the newly emerging country. Since 1831–1832 and the critique of the United States by Alexis de Tocqueville (1805–1859), we have been belabored for our money-grabbing, aggressive, materialistic individualism. Stephen Foster, in sentimental songs for adults, and Santa Claus, in gifts for children, offered us escape from ourselves. In terms of this purposeful if partially unconscious effort to create a new pattern, Santa Claus appears to serve a greater purpose than simply to represent a fanciful, mythological figure. He is the personification of the idealistic world we have tried to create for small children since he is supposed to magically arrive with whatever the child wants. This is just the reverse of what adults may expect from life in their competitive world. By supporting the myth of Santa, we express our own misgivings about the psychological satisfactions derived from our materialistic cultural system. This rationale for the function of Santa Claus may not seem entirely adequate, and yet it must be of some pertinence in the development of this pattern.

The emergence of Santa Claus as a unique personality demonstrates historically the way in which a new particular pattern may grow out of an older one. Both St. Nicholas and Santa Claus are supernatural gift-givers, but Santa Claus is a mythological figure whereas St. Nicholas had historical and religious origins. Particulars in the shift from one form to the other include Santa's arrival on the eve of December 25th rather than on the eve of December 6th, the horse-drawn wagon becoming a sleigh pulled by reindeer, and the appearance of a Dutch saint changing to that of the jolly, chubby, American form. The poem by Clement C. Moore and the Santa illustrations conceived by Thomas Nast helped to crystallize his image, and Santa Claus became a national figure whose patterned form has existed intact for a hundred years.

The development of our Santa Claus pattern illustrates certain qualities of patterning which apply far beyond this highly specific example. Note that the shift from a sacred religious personality to a secular folk hero was accomplished with only minor change in the individual's physical form. Thus religious symbols may be stripped of their meaning but still retain their basic form. The alteration of previously existing ideas and the resultant creation of something new is well illustrated by the 1822 Christmas poem which emerged from others published in 1815 and 1821 respectively. Furthermore, certain characteristics of St. Nicholas which were incompatible with the collective image of Santa Claus, such as leaving hay by the fireplace to feed his horses, were dropped or modified. In addition, Thomas Nast, who had the skills necessary to give visual form to Santa Claus, was becoming popular at the very time when we were striving for national identity, a critical combination of a willing and able man and a receptive cultural system. Thus, there are sense, reason, and order in the creation of Santa Claus, and these same qualities are basic in the development of any other patterns to be shared by men.

A SYSTEMIC PATTERN: TREATMENT OF ILLNESS   The examples of buttons and Santa Claus are specific and highly particular in their configuration because they represent relatively simple levels of patterning. At a more abstract level are systemic patterns, which integrate diverse particular patterns. In order to illustrate the nature of systemic patterns I have chosen the treatment of illness. In this instance my purpose is to demonstrate the interrelationships of diverse particular patterns which join to form a broader unit of cultural import.

A glance around the world of tribal peoples soon reveals that all peoples had a body of knowledge and lore about illness. Treatment of minor ills was undertaken by individuals or by shamans, both of whom used accepted herbs and so on as medicine. Illnesses thought to be of psychological origin were treated by shamans, who used their supernatural powers to effect cures. The most difficult illnesses to treat were those of unknown physiological or psychological dimensions, and these were not uncommon since until the late eighteenth century, curers were largely unaware of the nature of disease. Successful cures were achieved by utilizing traditional knowledge or by trial, error, and chance. Buried failures resulting from the practitioners' ignorance were not uncommon.

In eighteenth-century England and America it was widely believed that God had placed a specific cure for each disease in the region where the illness was most common. This theoretically provided Indian practitioners, using Indian medicines, with an advantage in treating diseases prevalent in America. In fact, an afflicted colonist might have preferred to be treated by an Indian healer. Belief in the efficacy of Indian medicines lingered long in the United States. In 1711 the first English patent granted to an American was for a corn product called "Tuscarora Rice." This, the first indigenous patent medicine, was sold as a treatment for consumption.

As knowledge of diseases and cures increased, the systemic pattern of treatment became greatly enlarged, and for the sake of brevity, I will limit my discussion to the use of patent medicines in the United States. Soon after the introduction of "Tuscarora Rice," innumerable other patent medicines thrived because they were well promoted, inexpensive, and better tasting than the medicines prescribed by physicians. The first nationwide advertising campaigns were conducted to sell such products, and the particular form of container in which they were sold or the distinctive label used to identify them often was patented with the government. The availability of patent medicines at a time when medical doctors were not only scarce but were often distrusted because of their limited knowledge and success in treatment, created a booming market. The alcoholic content of many such medicines was appealing, particularly since some brands were from forty to eighty proof but were represented as nonalcoholic. This helps to explain their great popularity in the mid-1800s when the temperance movement had gained momentum. From 1820 onward, the Indian became an increasingly important symbol of the strong, healthy, natural man; this was reflected in a Hiawatha hair restorer, a Creek consumptive cure, and a Kickapoo cure-all. In 1881 the Indian show became an intimate part of patent medicine salesmanship.

The large-scale dependence on patent medicines in the eighteenth and nineteenth centuries illustrates one part of the treatment pattern over the span of two centuries. Although particular brands of medicines might succeed or fail, the larger network of relationships, the pattern of patent medicines, remained reasonably constant for about two hundred years. In general terms, the patent medicine industry was noncumulative, for the medicines sold later were no improvement over the earlier forms. The only cumulative change was in the promotion of the medicines, and this became an increasingly sophisticated operation.

Toward the end of the century two factors led to a decline of the patent medicine market. The first was an increased acceptance of the germ theory of disease; the second was the passing in 1906 of the Pure Food and Drug Act, which removed many brands from the market at a time in which 50,000 different patent medicines were sold in the United States. Throughout the great patent medicine era in the United States the manufacturers and customers had been largely ignorant concerning the nature of disease, and these medicines offered at the very least a cheap psychological balm and at best a cure. Physicians likewise reflected a dimension of not knowing at that time. As the germ theory of disease gained acceptance, there came the realization that many patent medicines were fraudulently represented. Even with the increased knowledge, however, some people remained ignorant of the more objective judgments and continued to rely on patent medicines as cure-alls. Others experimented with new treatments prescribed by medical doctors while at the same time continuing with bottled balms. Such persons were attempting to learn for themselves the potentialities of both forms of curing. Still others accepted the denouncements of balms either because they had faith in scientific medicine or because they had objective information available to them about its merits. Finally, there were some persons who were aware of the merits of scientific medicine but refused, on an emotional basis, to accept it.

One patent medicine baron, David Hostetter, who died in 1888, left an estate valued at some eighteen million dollars. Although he was exceptionally successful as a seller of nostrums, he was just one among many men who accumulated great wealth in this market. The activities of Hostetter and his competitors were not random but were part of an orderly system which purportedly involved curing as well as making money. The more elementary components comprising this system involved specific medicinal formulas, manufacturing equipment, advertising techniques, distribution methods, and the actual sale of balms.

As there is order in the patent medicine dimension of the treatment of illness, there is an ordering in all aspects of behavior shared by groups of people. This cannot be seen readily, however, until the elements have been studied as representations of particular patterns, the particular patterns fitted into systemic patterns, and the systemic patterns understood in terms of the universals which they represent. After such an analysis, the interrelationships become apparent. The ways in which the temperance movement and the American Indian affected patent medicine acceptance serve as an example. Although such diverse elements in our culture today as birth control devices, Woody Guthrie phonograph records, and jet aircraft appear totally unrelated when each is viewed in isolation, a placement of each in its particular and systemic patterns would lead to an awareness of their ultimate interrelationships. In this way we may see the orderly integration of diverse aspects of shared human behavior.

PATTERNS AND EVOLUTION Particular and systemic patterns always emerge through a recombination of parts of older patterns to form new and uniquely configurated wholes, in which the components often have increased in complexity. Thus, the process underlying pattern formation is that of change. In the social and cultural aspects of human behavior such change may be labeled sociocultural evolution, and this may be defined as the tendency for social and cultural traits or elements, the component parts of specific patterns, to become increasingly complex and diverse through time. The meaning of evolution is not to be confused with that of progress. The latter implies a subjective evaluation in terms of recognized goals, whereas evolution is an objective concept based on a comparison of the number, arrangement, and complexity of traits.

Among the key ideas to be developed in this book are first, that human behavior is patterned at various levels of abstraction, and second, that patterns change through time with a tendency to move toward greater complexity, that is, evolve. Admittedly, other hypotheses have been offered to explain the modifications which occur in cultures. One thesis holds that change is a random, nonpatterned process without coherence or system. This is not a very popular notion nor does it appear to be very sensible. It implies that change is a haphazard process without order. Another explanation acceptable to many persons is that an all-powerful, concentrated supernatural force, that is, a god, created man and his world and that changes from the original pattern of creation have been effected by the god's intervention for reasons we do not know and probably should not probe. A combination of faith and scripture perpetuates such thinking. Some individuals who subscribe to this concept believe also that not only did man result from a special creation by a powerful deity, but that tribal peoples represent those who have fallen from the grace of that god. These hypotheses, because of their narrow applicability, will not be considered further. Rather, we shall concentrate on sociocultural evolution and our attempt to understand it as a viable process.

The implication of patterned change is that alterations in any element, from a button to an idea, stem from an orderly process leading to increased complexity. In our world today we see such a change when financial institutions such as insurance companies shift their work load from many human accountants to a few people operating complex computers. From one year to the next we see the development of greater concentrations of energy, as in rocket fuels, as well as a vast proliferation of increasingly complex technological products. The interrelated change in manufactures is markedly illustrated by the 150 variations possible in the 1968 model automobiles produced by Chrysler Corporation. When all the models and their accessory alternatives are calculated, some eight million different combinations emerge. It is of course possible to attribute these and all other changes to a random process or to divine intervention into our daily lives. However, an objective study of the data currently available indicates that the evolutionary approach to understanding changes in products associated with man is far more reasonable.

Cultural evolution has general and specific dimensions which serve as useful means for discussing the concept. General cultural evolution is the continuing development of culture as a total entity, whereas specific evolution is concerned with the alterations in particular cultures or particular cultural traits. Within the framework of general evolution we may consider the emergence of dwelling forms among all men through time, for example, or attempt to fathom the diverse usages of a broadly applicable development such as rotary motion. Specific evolution, by contrast, is concerned with how the bearers of a particular culture, such as the Hottentots or the Japanese, emerged through time as distinct isolates. It also deals with the development of a single article such as the spear or the mechanical clock as a specific evolutionary process. All the histories of such particular cultures and particular items merge within the all-embracing concept of general sociocultural evolution.

CULTURE AND SOCIETY AS CONCEPTS Among the individuals studying man, the word "culture" has a particular meaning which is not the definition listed first in the dictionary. Before 1843 the word "culture" meant to cultivate, and it continues to have the same meaning in "horticulture," or "to cultivate the soil." On this base the word "cultured," meaning a refinement of taste and manners, was developed. Cultivators, those that farmed, considered themselves refined enough to stand apart from noncultivators, who were hunters, fishermen, or collectors, and thus savages or barbarians. The word first assumed a particular anthropological meaning when it was used by the German ethnographer Gustav E. Klemm (1802–1867) in 1843, but it was not commonly employed in this sense in the United States until the early decades of the present century. The word "culture," to those who study man, means the lifeway of a population isolated in a particular sense and in a general sense means the total of all the lifeways of all peoples. The most critical characteristic of culture in either of these contexts is that it is learned, shared, and patterned behavior which forms an integrated system. Within this system particular constellations of traits cluster as particular patterns; these in turn are integrated with one another into systemic patterns which in their totality produce a cultural pattern that is particular and unique in its configuration. In these terms we may describe the particular culture of the Pomo Indians in California, the Yakut of Siberia, or any other people and see the specifics of their way of life without judging as "good" or "bad" whatever they happen to do or not do. When most of the varieties of culture become known, it becomes possible to compare them and arrive at a statement about culture in general terms.

To deal with complex cultures such as our own, it is helpful to identify the existing subcultures. Citizens of the United States share traits such as history, hotdogs, highways, bigotry, a national flag, and so on. However, regionally as well as within regions, there is a great deal of variation in certain traits or aspects of behavior, and because of this, secondary cultural characteristics have developed in the United States. In these terms there are such subcultural entities as the Pennsylvania Dutch, the southeastern sharecropper, the southwestern rancher, and the ghetto dweller.

Cultural patterns involve such features as the arrangements of people on the land, their subsistence means, and their technological involvements. The social side of culture involves the institutional means through which the people interact with one another. These include kinship systems, marital arrangements, family life, and political and religious patterns. A distinction between the social and cultural aspects may be seen in all areas involving learned and shared human behavior. In the realm of the supernatural, cultural aspects would include religious forms such as the types of churches or temples, and other material manifestations; the social dimensions would include roles of and relationships between believers and their leaders. Since culture cannot endure without people and people make up social units, it is usually most appropriate to speak of sociocultural behavior as it pertains to an established group of people.

BIASES AND BORROWINGS Because we live within a unique sociocultural system, we have a tendency to assume that all of our component patterns are largely products of our own culture, having sprung from native brains. Although we acknowledge having borrowed words from the French and zories from the Japanese, we tend to regard as national in origin any item now considered to be our own. One natural result of such thinking is that we feel superior to other peoples on the assumption that we have given them a great deal but have accepted very little in return. If such feelings are justified, they should be demonstrable with reference to something very ordinary in our lives, such as our clothing. It becomes informative, therefore, to historically consider the items of clothing worn in the United States.

The first item of apparel for a modern man is underwear. His shorts of today are derived from a similar but longer-legged undergarment worn by Europeans during the latter half of the twelfth century. Next are his trousers, a type of clothing form which originated among the riders of horses in the steppe country of Western Russia possibly as early as 3000 B.C. Trousers were popular among the Germanic peoples in the first century A.D. and probably were introduced into western Europe by these people during one of their earlier ventures westward. The modern form of trousers began to emerge in western Europe during the French Revolution (1789–1795) and was developed fully by the early decades of the nineteenth century. It is of incidental note that by the early 1800s trouser cuffs had been innovated by Englishmen, who turned up the bottom of their trouser legs on rainy days. The cuffed style was introduced in the United States when a visiting Englishman was caught in the rain on his way to a wedding in New York City. Buttoned shirts, derived from a tunic style which developed into an unbuttoned shirt, emerged first in medieval Europe. The necktie may be traced back to the chin cloths which Roman orators wore to protect their throats. The neckcloths which the Croatians wore into battle may have been an idea borrowed from the Romans, but in any case the cravat was added as an item of clothing among the French and English in the 1600s. When the standing collar points began to turn down over the cravat in the 1840s, a large bow tie was used in its place. This was narrowed and became a knotted tie of the modern form in England and in the United States shortly before 1900. The double-breasted coat made its first appearance in England about 1800, and in 1890 it had dropped the tails and looked much like the sports coat of today. The belt probably came into use at the same time as trousers. Socks of felt, or perhaps they were foot bandages, were known to the ancient Greeks, whereas sewn fabric socks were worn by Roman Empire times (30 B.C.–476 A.D.). Coarse stockings were pulled over the breeches by A.D. 1100 in England, became longer until the late 1500s, and then were shortened to below the knee and were most often made of silk or fine yarn. Finally, shoes were derived from the short Roman leather boots of the first century A.D.; however, modern forms did not begin to emerge until the time of the Crusades, when many Europeans walked much farther than they ever had before.

The clothing of a woman includes panty briefs or briefs which developed in the 1930s from longer forms of the previous decade. It was the French drawers and knickers which became shortened to panties by 1924, after which they began to assume their modern form. The corset developed from a sleeved bodice called a kirtle worn by women in medieval Europe. The kirtle became a constricting garment when it came to be laced tightly and reinforced with sew-in strips of iron, steel, or whalebone. The corset reached from shoulder to hip during the Victorian period in England (1837–1901), but it had developed into a two-piece style in France by that time. The upper part had become known as a brassiere by 1912, and this French word was shortened to bra by 1937. The bra served as a bust-flattener in the 1920s but has since moved in the opposite direction. The lower part, called a girdle, was changed as early as 1911 when its support became less rigid and was provided by vulcanized rubber cloth rather than inserted stiffening strips of bone or metal. Undertunics were popular among Greek women about 1200 B.C., eventually came to be adopted by the Saxons, and emerged as petticoats among the sixteenth-century Venetians, from whom the French and English borrowed the idea. The modern fitted slip, cut on the bias, was developed in France during the 1920s. Blouses were worn by ninth-century English women, but they were much longer than the modern forms. Although contemporary types were a part of the garb of seventeenth-century Russian women, they were not introduced into the United States and England until about 1900. By 2000 B.C. the Semites and Babylonians wore tunics over the lower part of the body, and the Franks of Europe wore jumpers by the fifth century A.D. However, modern skirts, closely fitted and ending at the waist, did not originate until about 1800 in the United States, and they did not become popular until around 1910. The prototype of women's hose is the same as men's socks; both can be traced to the earlier socks or stockings sewn from fabric and later knitted.

Even this brief presentation illustrates that our clothing forms have a history that is much older than that of our country, and despite all of our emphasis on dress, the changes which we have made have been only stylistic in nature. "To dress American" would result in naked men and women. For all of our inventiveness we still follow the patterns set in Europe for clothing and have made no revolutionary inventions nor many lasting modifications. Thus, our cultural heritage with respect to clothing is un-American, and we would find the same to be true for many diverse aspects of our culture if we took the time to trace their origins.

ETHNOCENTRISM It is not difficult to understand the narrow viewpoint of stay-at-home tribal peoples. They are provincial and have a perspective which is even more limited than our own. If we were to ask hypothetical primitives of tribe X, who happened to be wearers of clothes, "What is the origin of your clothing?" the answer would most likely be, "We have always had it," which is in a sense true. Although many other societies had contributed to their clothing forms originally, such influences had faded beyond recall. Tribe X might have some verbal history about their garments as well as stories or myths on the subject, but information retained solely by means of oral tradition usually is very limited. Just as the members of tribe X lack historical information about their clothing, they also lack a historical perspective for other aspects of their culture and society. Furthermore, since very few changes are completed within the lifetime of any particular person in such societies, this leads each generation to assume that everything has always been very much as it is in their time.

If the members of tribe X follow the norm among primitives, they will consider their tools, weapons, family life, political system and so on, as unique to themselves. Since the people who live closest to them generally occupy a similar ecological niche, they bear a similar, although far from identical, lifeway; therefore the X people must exaggerate the quality of their differences from their neighbors in order to maintain their distinctness. In so doing, they assert the belief that they are racially and culturally superior to their neighbors. Among many tribal peoples this attitude is well reflected in the name that they have for themselves. For example, we call a group of primitives in northern North America, Eskimos; this name, originated by certain Indians to the south of the Eskimos, means "Eaters of Raw Flesh." However, the Eskimos' own name for themselves is not Eskimos but is Inupik, meaning "Real People." By their name they provide a contrast between themselves and other groups; the latter might be "people" but are never "real." This concept of superiority is not limited to the primitive, however. When traveling abroad, a citizen of the United States rarely need identify his homeland, because his clothing, cameras, and general bearing give away his tribal identity, although admittedly he might be confused with a West German. If asked, however, he will most likely say, "I am an

American." The implication is not that the individual is an inhabitant of the New World, from any one of the three Americas, north, middle, or south. Instead, the statement is expected to convey the meaning that the speaker is a citizen of the United States. The bias which causes the "United Statian" to consider his countrymen as the only Americans worthy of identification as such indicates that the concept of tribal superiority extends into the modern scene.

A contrast of "me" with "you" or "us" with "them" may be simply an objective assessment of the differences between cultures. If, however, the distinction is of the boastful type ascribed to the Eskimo and the citizen of the United States, it is based on subjective evaluations of similarities and differences. To hold one's own cultural ways up as the norm for measuring those of others is to reflect a bias in favor of one's own. In some respects this is desirable, for it gives one a full and meaningful sense of identity and assurance. In other ways it is harmful because it encourages intolerance. A bias in favor of one's own culture is termed ethnocentrism, and if one's culture is perfect in all contexts, an ethnocentric view is reasonable. If, however, there are areas in which one might profitably learn from other peoples, then in the long run an ethnocentric stance may be detrimental to one's entire way of living. This underlies the anthropological recommendation to avoid hardening of the cultural arteries by at least sampling other ways of life through traveling abroad or reading about other peoples. To assert dogmatically that one's own ways are the only right ones may spell doom and destruction, or at least despair and frustration. In this rapidly changing world each people is likely to have at least something of value to offer, not necessarily for the survival of a particular form of culture, but more importantly, for the continuation of culture itself.

ORDER AND CHANGE   An empirical generalization may be made that order exists everywhere in the natural and man-made worlds. This observation suggests a galaxy-wide law that pattern is everywhere. A second law is that there is no fixity in either natural or human ways. The central Australian natives probably have remained relatively constant in their cultural behavior longer than any other modern primitives, but their archaic culture happened to survive because of the geographically isolated continent that they occupied. Although such exceptions do occur, change is the norm. Clothing styles come and go; gods are conceived and later discarded; and animal species evolve. Form is altered by change, and as the changes become more involved, the general trend is toward an increased complexity in social and cultural form. This evolutionary process, as it occurs in sociocultural systems, leads to increased organization, greater heterogeneity, and higher energy concentrations. The process is natural, orderly, and continuous, although the tempo may vary with time and substance. In the balance of this book certain dimensions of ordered change will be explored so that we may better understand ourselves and other peoples by seeing something of where we have been, what we are, and the direction in which we appear to be moving.

2

TIME AND SPACE

Try for a moment to conceive of yourself after negating all thoughts of time and space. Inducing this mental state would place you in an uncertain limbo, which is doubtfully livable, at least in this world. Thus, time and space are qualities in the very nature of life, and all conceivable units known to man possess these referents. It is by probing thoughts about these matters, from the primitive and modern worlds, that we may come to realize the essence of our concept of reality. I am concerned with the ways in which the concepts of time and space as dimensions of distance have entered our thinking. In this context distance includes the time interval between two events as well as the degree of spatial separation between two points or surfaces. The temporal and spatial nature of distance is implicitly recognized by tribal and civilized man alike, but the ideas have become refined in our technologically-directed culture for a unique degree of precision. Our views about distance have led us to questions never before asked concerning the nature of the world and man's place in it.

QUALITIES OF TIME   To understand the nature of time it is helpful to distinguish it as relative or as absolute. For time to be conceived in absolute or scientific terms the units can not be variable. They must remain constant, be of equal duration, and be assigned to a consistent scale. By contrast, relative time lacks the precise units of duration and does not have a constant scale. One form of relative time is cyclical and includes events which recur in a definite sequence but in a noncumulative manner. The planting, growing, and harvesting seasons are relative and cyclical since they consistently recur in the same order. The yearly arrival of salmon at their spawning streams, the spring migration of whales, the days, the nights—each is repetitious annually but has no absolute beginning or end point.

Many primitive peoples think of time in these terms of general relativity, but they also speak of the very remote past when gods, spirits, or other races of men lived on earth. This would be mythological or magical time, which again is relative. Since unusual events are time-markers among men and in nature, we may also conceive of the category "catastrophic time" among primitives. The time of the great flood, the earthquake, the year that the snow never left the ground, or the time of a great victory—these would be relative to each other, not cyclical and yet in a sense cumulative, since one event may be known to have occurred before or after another. When a catastrophic chronology is expanded to include events of a more mundane nature, it becomes oral history, or a record of unique events in a proper or imagined sequence. Among Polynesians, the tales about their voyages from one island to another, the names of the prominent persons involved, the great hurricanes encountered are combined in such a record. Again, the Inca of Peru possessed such an oral history about the founding and development of their empire. The time involved in such an oral history usually is subdivided in terms of the lives of key personalities in the record, and although it thus remains relative, time is thought of in a more precise manner than it had been previously. For our purposes, it is not important that oral history often blends imperceptibly into mythology; such history is important because it represents a fixed sequence.

SAULTEAUX INDIAN TIME A short distance east of Lake Winnipeg in Manitoba, Canada, lives a group of Indians called the Saulteaux, probably better known under the more general designations of Ojibwa or Chippewa. Their aboriginal conception of time, which is well reported, was primarily cyclical, although the system also expressed cumulative time within a restricted framework. According to the mythology of these hunters and fishermen, when the world was new and before the present order on earth, there was an era during which some of the creatures known today, such as the beaver and mosquito, were the size of monsters. Most of these monstrous beings became extinct, although a few lived on in their original form. In the past too a flood and other world-shaping events occurred, but these episodes were not conceived in sequential terms within their mythological tradition. One probable reason for chronology playing a minor role in their reckoning of the distant past is that certain elements of it were continuous into the present. Some of the monsters still remained alive, and more importantly, the great immortal spirits who were in existence when the earth was young continued to aid men. Thus, there was a sameness from the beginning to the present. The Saulteaux did with some competence order historical events back as far as one hundred and fifty years ago, but again this was not in our familiar style. Their historical chronology was made possible by referring to signal events of general or, more often, personal importance, such as the first missionary's arrival at a village, or the time when one's father's father frequented a particular hunting area. Since the referent was most often personal and unique, the events involved in such a chronology were not generally of common interest. An individual's age, in a like manner, was not expressed in terms of years or "winters" but was marked by different stages in his life from that of a young child to an aged person. As might be expected, a "year" had no fixed beginning or end; it might be calculated by starting with the moon then current or at almost any point in the lunar series. To the Saulteaux a "moon" meant the time from one full moon to the next; there were thirteen of these periods, of which twelve were named. The moons correlated roughly with six named seasons: spring, summer, fall, "Indian Summer," early winter, and late winter. No named "days" or "weeks" existed in their thoughts, but they divided the solar day into twelve units. These were of unequal duration, with seven occurring before noon. Dawn, with its first sunlight, was followed by "before coming out from the trees [the sun]," when objects could be seen at some distance. As the sun lightened the treetops, it was "red shining [reflected] light," and so on until the sun was seen as "disappearing underneath day." Darkness was either night or "nearly half [the] night," and thus day and night were separate temporal units. It was nights or "sleeps" in which distances traveled were measured.

In Saulteaux time descriptions, we find familiar words, but they are employed in ways alien to our thinking. The major similarity between the Indian system and ours is that both may calculate relative time within a personal frame of reference. Beyond this point their system seems inexact, and this clearly is one of its major disadvantages in our terms. However, given their living conditions, the pattern for plotting time was systematic and very reasonable. Life among the

Saulteaux was focused on daily hunting and fishing activities, and the uncertainty of their subsistence success resulted in a rather precarious existence. Exact calculations were insignificant in either long or short time periods. Each span of daylight was important to them as a unit for survival. In a like manner their oral history had survival pertinence, and yet it was unnecessary that it be chronologically specific.

MEASURING OUR TIME   During the eighteenth dynasty in Egypt, centering around 1300 B.C., relative time was measured by diverse means and with varying degrees of exactness. The rise of the Nile River waters in June and their recession in October had become the basis for determining cyclical time, and a calendar based on day counts recorded relative and cumulative periods. The water clock offered a rather precise means for the calculation of brief time periods and was used to divide day and night into twelve hours each. A water clock consisted of a bowl with a hole in the base and an hour scale graduated along the sides. Such clocks did not record absolute time, however, since no two offered exactly the same measurement. The Egyptians of this era also plotted the time of the day with sun-dials, whereas nighttime hours were calculated by following the movement of stars.

The ability to measure time with considerable accuracy was developed by the Babylonians. Their business months of thirty days each had a correlate with lunar months of thirty days each (really 27.3216 days), defined on the basis of movements of star constellations during this span of time over a thirty-degree arc. Their twelve months of thirty days each do not add up exactly to an astronomical year; if they did, the year would be based on a three-hundred-and-sixty-degree circle. The division into months was important in determining when to plant crops, but because the planting month eventually strayed from the season, it was necessary to intercalate an arbitrary month periodically. In Babylonia by 380 B.C. a rule was formulated for a fixed intercalation so that in a cycle of nineteen years there were seven years with thirteen lunar months and twelve years with twelve lunar months; this cycle later came to be termed Metonic.

The twenty-four-hour count for day and night acquired from the Egyptians was further refined by the division of each hour into sixty minutes, a concept based originally on a Babylonian measurement of distance. This combination provided the units for the precise time scale which eventually emerged in Medieval Europe. During the Medieval era civil life was regulated on a twenty-four-hour scale; Medieval church time, however, was canonical, with the hours of unequal span because they were based on the time required to recite particular prayers and devotions. Water clocks with vastly improved accuracy were developed in Europe and lasted until the eighteenth century, although they began to fade from vogue following the emergence of mechanical clocks in the late thirteenth century.

The early mechanical clocks, which most often were housed in a special clock tower appended to a church establishment, were of two types. One form simply struck the hour, but the other had a face with twelve or twenty-four hour units marked on it. The faced clock provided a visual image of time in terms of the distance between marks. These clocks became relatively accurate only after the problem of making geared wheels had been solved successfully. The drive for mechanical clocks was provided by suspended weights which set geared wheels into motion. In order to prevent the gears from accelerating their rate of speed, another essential feature was an oscillatory escapement mechanism. Mechanical clocks and firearms were the first complex mechanisms made from metal and served as precursors for later automatic machinery.

An effort to standardize time was made in France in 1370, but the first really accurate clock, the refined pendulum clock, did not appear until 1657. By the late 1700s timepieces were highly accurate so long as they remained stable and fixed. However, in this great era of explorations, mariners could not successfully use such clocks on ships. At sea a navigator could calculate latitude—the north-south dimension of the earth's surface—by the stars, and local time could be determined accurately by observing when the sun was at its apex daily. However, the calculation of longitude—the east-west dimension of the earth's surface—required an accurate clock for the correlation of local time with that at the zero meridian in Greenwich, England. Since local time is an hour earlier than Greenwich time for each fifteen degrees east of the zero meridian and an hour later for the same distance west, if a shipboard clock was in error as little as five seconds, the miscalculation of distance could be as much as one and a third miles.

To map newly discovered areas of the world an extremely accurate timepiece was essential, and nowhere was the desire for such a device greater than in England. In 1714 the government established the Board of Longitude to test new marine clocks, and 20,000 pounds were to be awarded to anyone developing a timepiece that would remain accurate within half a degree on a trip between the British Isles and the West Indies. This offer of so great a sum for a clock is an excellent and historically early example of a reward being used to encourage the innovation of a technological device. This precedent would be followed often in industrial societies as they faced critical mechanical problems.

A central figure in the development of a highly accurate mariner's clock was John Harrison (1693–1776), the son of a Yorkshire carpenter. He was trained in his father's trade, but he specialized in making clocks. He designed a new clock for ships in 1728, and with the aid of money from a patron he built it by 1735. The clock was tested on a trip to Lisbon in 1736, and while it did not satisfy the government requirements completely, Harrison was awarded 500 pounds to continue his work. He completed a second clock in 1739 but was personally dissatisfied with the result, and it was not formally tested. The following year Harrison began to craft a third clock, and it occupied his attention for seventeen years. At the end of this time he was satisfied with its accuracy, but he spent another two years making it into a more compact model. When this clock was tested in 1761 on a trip to Jamaica, it was off only one and a half seconds. Unfortunately, Harrison did not receive his reward until ten years and another clock later; within another three years he died.

THE TIME OF THE PAST The quality of time always has existed, and man probably intellectualized about its relative nature early in his emergence. In the process he would have discovered a patterning in the natural world which we call temporal. Time must almost have been forced into the thinking of man since its relative dimensions are so apparent in the days and nights, the months, and the seasons. With an increased interest in duration and sequence came the establishment of symbolic units which expressed time. These units could be precise only after the invention of mechanical means for recording time's passage. Water and tower clocks and the mariner's clocks of John Harrison all represent major steps in this process. After time was abstractly conceived and then accurately measured, it was possible for man to think beyond specific events at particular places and thus begin to relate anything and everything within a chronological sequence. It became recognized that time is a quality embodied in living or nonliving things, and that in its expansiveness it is beyond direct human control. Once precisely conceived, the idea of time led inevitably to a different view of the past. Before this era, events had been ordered in terms of the remote or recent past in a very general and often inaccurate way, but now the relationships within this past were recordable in more meaningful terms. A knowledge of minutes and hours from clocks, and of days, months, and years from calendars soon would lead to questions about the duration of earthly time. The almost obvious question to follow was that of the age of man on earth; this query is perhaps one of the most penetrating that man will ever ask about himself.

In the days of ancient Greece, Herodotus reflected on historical consciousness, and this awareness was carried into the thinking of later Arabic scholars. Yet it was Europeans in the late Middle Ages who first developed a distinct pattern of historical interests. To select one person to represent the apogee of time awareness at the culmination of this era would be to choose James Ussher (1581–1656), an Irish archbishop in the Anglican Church and one of the great biblical scholars. In 1650 he published *Annals of the Ancient and New Testaments,* in which a chronology of biblical events was advanced. Ussher concluded that the world had been created in 4004 B.C., and by 1701 this judgment was printed as a marginal note in the authorized version of the Bible. Another biblical scholar offered a calculation even more precise than that of the archbishop. According to Dr. John Lightfoot (1602–1675), Vice-Chancellor of the University of Cambridge, the year was indeed 4004 B.C., but more specifically the time was October 23rd at 9 a.m. Once the date of the world's beginning had been thus expounded, the interest in time periods shifted to a debate over whether Adam and Eve had been expelled from the Garden of Eden within a few hours after the creation or after seven days.

Archbishop Ussher's book was reprinted into the eighteenth century, which suggests the durability of his authoritative views. Between the seventeenth and nineteenth centuries most English scholars agreed that divine foresight best explained the orderliness in the world and that their task was rather to describe and fathom its dimensions. The theologian and the natural philosopher were not in conflict with one another, for their findings simply reinforced mutual convictions. This was an era when many men developed broad interests in the nature of the world and attempted to apply their knowledge in order to better conditions among men. Great scientific societies were being organized to disseminate the rapidly accumulating body of knowledge. Since the earth yielded so much to man, the land itself was studied for purposes both practical and scientific. By 1790 the reality of the great biblical flood was considered verified by seashells found high on mountains. The creation as recorded in Genesis remained fully acceptable, as was the archbishop's creation date, and the fauna and flora of the world were thought permanent and immutable. It was not agreed whether all things had been created at one time or whether there had been a series of creations, but this was not a great issue at that time.

In 1795, James Hutton (1726–1797) published his book *Theory of the Earth*, and a new phase of geological inquiry dawned. Hutton proposed a synthetic view of empirical data; he was an early volcanist, a label applied to those geologists stressing the role of volcanic action in forming the earth's surface. By studying the present he inferred the past, and while he noted that earthly changes were slow, implying that a great deal of time would have been necessary for present conditions to emerge, he did not challenge the accepted chronology nor was he concerned with ultimate origins. The empirical approach of Hutton was important also in the development of William Buckland's catastrophic view of geology. Buckland (1784–1856) too accepted biblical accounts about the earth's creation and considered that his studies served to illuminate the works of the "Divine Engineer," but he felt that the six days of creation should not be taken literally. His major contribution, made between 1820 and 1830, was to establish a sequential chronology of animal creation on the basis of stratigraphic evidence. First came the fishes, then amphibians, next reptiles, and finally mammals. Since no human bones were recovered, it was presumed that man was very recently created by God.

Modern geology emerged with the publication in 1830 of volume one of *Principles of Geology* by Charles Lyell (1797–1875). The key to this integrative synthesis was that temporal continuity best explained the earth-modifying processes. Lyell concluded that the rates of earth building and those of erosion were the same throughout time and that they continued to operate in a very slow manner. As he developed his uniformitarian thesis in a three-volume work, Lyell concluded that species were created at different times and were immutable, and he further proposed that there had been great floods but no single worldwide flood. Although he never directly attacked scriptural doctrines, his work led to the disputes on which the god and science war soon would be based.

TIMELY CONCLUSIONS Time as a systemic pattern has long and short dimensions, as reflected in years and hours. Historically, years first were defined with exactness through astronomical observations, whereas hourly precision came later with the development of a mechanically oriented technology. During the development of our time consciousness precise measurements of absolute, long-term time began to be achieved during the latter part of the eighteenth century.

This led to new interest in, and interpretations of, the earth's most remote eras. During the same period the remote spaces of the world were also becoming known, and the primitive peoples found they were to add yet another dimension to the nature of being human.

EARTHLY SPACE The concept of distance includes ideas of both time and space, with the critical dimension of time being duration. When time is thought of as a form of measurement between two points on the earth's surface, it becomes space, and the time which elapses between the movement from one geographical spot to another becomes a measurement of distance. Involvement with geographical space may be self-experienced or vicarious, drawn from the experience of others. When of the latter category, spatial concepts may require presentation in graphic, oral, or written form. It is in its graphic representation, as conveyed by maps, that space is best illustrated. Map-making abilities are shared by many peoples, both tribal and civilized. Highly symbolic maps drawn in sand were common among the aboriginal people in central Australia, and lattice-work navigational charts of islands and water currents were commonplace in Polynesia. Eskimos at the time of historic contact were able to draw maps for explorers depicting sizeable areas in accurate proportions.

YUROK INDIAN SPATIAL CONCEPTS We conceive of space primarily in terms of four cardinal directions. Other peoples often orient themselves in similar terms but add the directions "up" and "down," making a system of six cardinals. Neither system is inherently superior; they are simply different ways in which to orient oneself in space. A marked departure from these directional systems is the one of the salmon-fishing Yurok Indians who live in northern California. At the time of historic contact the Yurok thought that the earth was flat, approximately circular, and surrounded by water, beyond which was a sea of pitch with islands along one quadrant. The entire expanse was covered with a vault of sky which was not conceived of as fixed but which rose and fell into the sea, causing breakers along the seashore. The geese had their own particular opening in the sky, a "sky-hole" through which they flew beyond the sky or entered into this world. To the west and north, in our directional terms, were the earthly homes of supernaturals; these existed on islands at the edge of the sea of pitch. The gently undulating land mass rested on water and had its geographical center in the heart of Yurok country, near where the

Trinity and Klamath rivers join. From this point the earth extended for about seventy-five miles in all directions (Figure 4). The Yurok

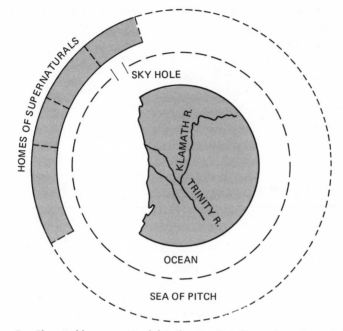

Figure 4. *The world as conceived by the Yurok Indians of northern California (After T. T. Waterman, "Yurok Geography," Univ. of Calif. Publ. in Am. Archaeology and Ethnology, v. 16, no. 5, 1920).*

were unaware that water bordered their country only on one side because they did not travel inland far enough to reach the assumed eastern limits of the earth nor did they welcome strangers. These Indians were primarily river dwellers, and directions were conceptualized in terms of water flow in the Klamath River, with upstream and downstream as the two alternatives. Because the Pacific was reached by traveling downstream, the coast north of the Klamath River mouth was viewed as a further extension of the downstream direction. It might be felt that it would be difficult to orient oneself in more than a vague manner within their area, which was true. However, these Indians also had names for a great many specific geographical locations, especially along the banks of the Klamath River, and this made it possible to designate locations by using particular place-names rather than directional terms.

SYMBOLIZING EARTHLY SPACE   Among the earliest maps found on the course toward literate Western societies is a clay one made by a Babylonian in about 3800 B.C. It outlined a broad area of the Near East, and its complexity indicated that it was not the first map produced. Later some Greek philosophers who were interested in abstract cartography experimented with symbolizing the shape of the earth rather than simply representing known relationships between geographical areas. By the sixth century B.C. the Greeks had drawn maps of all of the known world, and two hundred years later they grappled with the problem of including a line of orientation on maps. Possibly the first memorable name in cartography is that of Eratosthenes (276–195 B.C.), who was in charge of the famous library at Alexandria. He proposed that a number of parallel orienting lines be added to maps and that these be at unequal distances from each other. However, he is more renowned for the land survey he made from Syene to Alexandria, the first study to demonstrate the roundness of the earth. The most famous scholar of ancient Alexandria, Ptolemy (Klaudios Ptolemaios, A.D. 87–150), was known for his *Geographia*. This compendium of astronomical, historical, and geographical information was lost to history, but copies which were made from the original at a later date are available. It is not at all certain how much of the material Ptolemy actually wrote, and neither is it known whether the original included maps. It would seem that he utilized the concept of a prime meridian, calculated coordinates in degrees, and located places in terms of longitude and latitude. By the thirteenth century *Geographia* included eight books, but only two are attributed to Ptolemy. The other books were authored by three or four persons after Ptolemy's time. It was this work in its entirety that constituted the prime source of geographical knowledge in the Middle Ages. Since the Medieval church had no objections to cartography, Christian versions of maps were produced. A popular form was the circular map of the T-O tradition, with the T inside the O; these were known also as wheel maps. On one style of T-O map, east was at the top of the circle, and water masses were represented on the T. The crossbar of the T was the Don River on the right and the Nile River on the left, whereas the vertical of the T was the Mediterranean Sea. Thus, Asia was the eastern land mass, with Europe on the north and Africa to the south in this highly schematic presentation (Figure 5). This was only one of the Medieval forms of maps in which imagination and cartography vied in diverse combinations.

The long-term importance of Ptolemy's *Geographia* is illustrated by the fact that it was translated into Latin by 1406, but soon afterward it was realized that the accompanying maps were quite inaccurate. Discrepancies were found when new maps were made following overland travels in Europe and sea voyages from the continent. Coast pilots, which combined descriptions of voyages with sailing directions; sea charts, and books about islands and their locations made specific and important contributions. These, coupled with the existence of an improved magnetic compass and the introduction of printing, made it possible for accurate maps to be compiled and distributed rather widely. In the year 1492 the first globe was produced, and in less than a decade after the initial discoveries by Columbus, the information he obtained was incorporated on world maps.

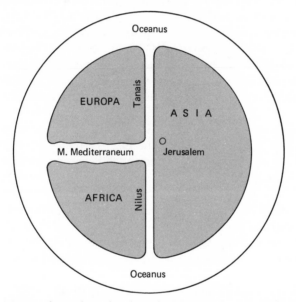

Figure 5.   A map dating from the eleventh century in the T-O tradition (Courtesy of George Philip and Son Limited, from W. W. Jervis, The World in Maps, 1938).

DISCOVERING NEW PEOPLES   The cumulative improvement of maps and the production of globes is in part a record of European exploration and technology. An important aspect of this expansion was that finding new lands usually meant the discovery of new peoples, except on the Antarctic continent. By Europeans the exotic peoples were first thought of as bizarre and monstrous beings whose imagined ways were a source of amazement. The primitives' physical appearance, their garb, and their customs provided intriguing glimpses into ways of life which at first seemed astoundingly different from those of any of the diverse peoples in Europe or nearby. New World peoples generally were considered savages, barbarians, or naturals, although by some they came to be thought of as either ignoble or noble in their savage ways. Tribal peoples taken to Europe actually were mobbed when they appeared in the street because people were so anxious to catch a glimpse of them. Firsthand acquaintance with an aborigine was impossible for most Europeans, but published accounts about the strange peoples who lived in faraway places were available and very popular.

At first, before the great maritime expansion of the fifteenth and sixteenth centuries, the discovery of peoples was of little general interest to Europeans. Later tribal peoples emerged as a timely subject for observation and presentation. Once the differences in human ways became recognized we have the first developmental steps toward the anthropological concept of culture. However, even by the 1830s there was comparatively little understanding of primitive peoples by most relatively sophisticated Europeans. The material presented below is one example of four Fuegians, from the tip of South America, who were taken to England in 1830. The case is presented in some detail because it represents a lengthy encounter between representatives of disparate cultures which was written by relatively unbiased and literary men. It illustrates the degree of cultural separation between Europeans and primitives which existed in the recent past.

Early 1830 found Robert Fitzroy, captain of the English survey vessel *Beagle,* and his crew at the southern tip of South America. Here among the islands that comprise Tierra del Fuego, they had frequent contact with the local Indians, the Fuegians if they are identified only in a general sense. According to one account, a small boat from the *Beagle* was stolen, and in order to encourage its return, hostages were seized from among the Fuegians. At night all except three children escaped, and one of these, a girl about nine years of age, so charmed the crew that they decided to keep her aboard after they had released the other two. She acquired the name Fuegia Basket, and she was treated with kindness and affection. While the *Beagle* was still in the same area, it was visited by other Fuegians about two months later. From among these visitors the captain decided to take back with him a man in his early twenties who seemed willing to leave; this man subsequently was named York Minster. Before sailing from Fireland the commander supposedly obtained a boy, about fourteen years old, from other visitors in exchange for a pearl button, and he was named Jemmy Button. A fourth individual, a male who came to be called Boat Memory, also was taken, and soon afterward the *Beagle* departed for England with the four Fuegians aboard.

Fitzroy decided to educate the captives in England and then return them to their homeland. He hoped that once back among their own people his Anglicized Fuegians would be able to introduce civilized ways to the others. It is fitting to mention that the Fuegians may justly be numbered among the Indians with the least complex culture in all of the Americas. Those captured were from a group of maritime hunters and fishermen who subsisted largely on diverse forms of sea life. Their inventory of material items consisted of highly portable and technically simple tools, weapons, and containers. Clothing was minimal, and housing was provided by temporary brush or skin shelters. Only when a dead whale happened to drift ashore was there enough food to enable more than a few families to remain together in one locality for any length of time.

On the trip to England the Fuegians began to learn English from the crew. After reaching England, each was vaccinated against small-pox as soon as possible; but despite this precaution Boat Memory died of the disease. The three survivors were settled for nearly a year as boarders with a minister who lived near London, and they attended a school which he managed. York Minster was not a very diligent pupil, but the other two seem to have done well enough. At the request of King William IV the Indians were granted an audience, and both the king and the queen found Fuegia Basket engaging. The queen removed her lace cap and placed it on the head of Fuegia, and the king gave her a ring from his finger as well as money for a trousseau. Late in 1831 preparations were made by Fitzroy to sail the *Beagle* back to South America. At the end of the year the ship departed, and on board were the Fuegians as well as Charles Darwin, who served as the naturalist.

Darwin discussed the returnees but not in great detail in his journal of the voyage. He found York Minster to be reserved, taciturn, and morose, although "violently passionate" when excited. York obviously was determined to marry Fuegia as soon as they had returned. Jemmy Button was temperamental, but he was well liked by everyone because he was merry as well as sympathetic. Jemmy was something of a dandy, being prone to look at himself in a mirror quite often. He also made certain that his hair was always neatly cut and his shoes well polished. Fuegia Basket was described as a "nice, modest, reserved" young girl who was quick to learn. From watching the Indians and questioning them and from the observations of others,

Darwin concluded that the Fuegians had no government, no family affections, and no religion. On the other hand, he did not consider them to be much more superstitious than some of the *Beagle's* sailors.

The *Beagle* arrived back in Fireland late in 1832, and early the next year the Indians were returned to the area in which Jemmy's relatives lived, the locale where they all wanted to settle. Jemmy's mother and brothers soon arrived, and Darwin described the reunion between Jemmy and his mother. "The meeting was less interesting than that between a horse, turned out into a field, when he joins an old companion. There was no demonstration of affection; they simply stared for a short time at each other; and the mother immediately went to look after her canoe." After seeing to it that the returned captives were settled, the *Beagle* party left to survey a nearby area. By the time they returned about a week later, many of the possessions that Jemmy and York had brought back with them had been taken by other Fuegians. It was with considerable sadness that Fitzroy left his former charges to their own devices and departed a few days later. Nearly a year passed before the *Beagle* again returned to the area where the Fuegians had been left, and no one appeared to greet the ship at first. Then as Darwin writes, "Soon a canoe, with a little flag flying, was seen approaching, with one of the men in it washing the paint off his face. This man was poor Jemmy,—now a thin haggard savage, with long disordered hair, and naked, except a bit of blanket round his waist. We did not recognize him till he was close to us; for he was ashamed of himself, and turned his back to the ship. We had left him plump, fat, clean, and well dressed;—I never saw so complete and grievous a change." After Jemmy had been clothed again, he dined with the captain and told about what had happened during the past year. He had lost all of his property to York, who had stolen it one night while camped with Jemmy and his mother. During the past year Jemmy had been once again learning to speak his native language; he had built himself a canoe and had acquired a young wife. Apparently it was affection for his wife that dissuaded him from returning to England. Before leaving the ship Jemmy was again given a great deal of property and the best wishes of the entire ship's company. As the *Beagle* sailed away forever, Jemmy lighted a signal fire as his last gesture to his English friends.

Intimate contact with the Fuegian trio ends here, but information concerning them was obtained later. Some years after their return, Jemmy Button seemingly was the instigator of a massacre of six missionaries who had founded a local station in 1859; other missionaries persuaded the British government not to take retaliatory action against him. York was murdered because he had killed another man; after York's death, Fuegia Basket remarried. She was old and near death when last seen in 1883.

From Fitzroy's experiment, the Fuegians' actions and reactions, and Darwin's comments, it becomes possible to visualize the nineteenth-century European views toward tribal peoples. Fitzroy considered his captives to be from one of the most backward tribes of savages, but he felt that they could be civilized. In a figurative sense, and in a literal one as applied to Fuegia and Jemmy when first captured, primitive peoples were thought to have the mental abilities of children, but also like children, they were considered capable of learning. The notion that adults among savages were at the same mental level as the children in civilized societies is an idea retained by many persons to this day. Such a view is held by people who have had little or no contact with tribal peoples or whose familiarity with tribal peoples, although sustained, has been superficial. After a missionary, ethnographer, or other person comes to know tribal peoples well, meaning particularly after he has learned their language, he realizes that their minds are anything but childlike. Primitives have complex ideological systems, with nuances of meanings which could be appreciated by a Western philosopher. Their knowledge of plants or animals may in many respects be compared to the systematic approaches of botanists and zoologists. Admittedly, they could not verbalize about concepts with which they had no prior contact, but within their own realm of thinking were abstractions for which they had adequate terms. The most likely reason for Europeans to think of primitives as children is that the people discovered are forced to learn the language of the discoverers, and without a thorough understanding of this contact language, the ideas they can express are likely to be simple. In addition, individuals among primitives, as elsewhere, have different degrees of intelligence, and dealing with a few such persons may give an inaccurate view of the group as a whole.

On the positive side of learning among the Fuegians, Darwin noted that after rather brief exposure to Portuguese and Spanish, Fuegia rapidly acquired some knowledge of these languages, and that a year after his return Jemmy had taught some English to all of his tribe. Fitzroy had felt that by taking the Fuegians to England he was offering them the blessings of civilization, but their exposure was relatively brief and was limited in breadth. Of their three years among the English about half of the time was spent among sailors on the *Beagle*, and this could not have been an optimum setting for learning Western ways. What they did acquire rather quickly was the veneer of another culture, but they could hardly be considered a test case for the civilizing of tribal peoples. Yet it was limited exposures such as these and the false illusion that simply clothing an aborigine in European garb could inwardly transform him which led many Westerners to decide that primitive people in general were incapable of learning civilized ways. This was the attitude assumed by Fitzroy after he saw the Fuegians readapt to their homeland. Darwin considered the captives as likeable and interesting subjects, but in a sense he thought them more human-like than human. His conclusions were drawn from the presumption that they had no government, no religion, and so on, and yet these judgments were incorrect since Darwin was unable to fully understand his informants. He felt that the egalitarian nature of Fuegian society kept the people in a simple state, and he doubted that they could be civilized.

What the Fuegians thought of the English is hard to determine, but there are indications that they regarded their discoverers as childlike except for their technological sophistication. A good example of English gullibility, in Fuegian eyes, was their acceptance of the Fuegians' tales of cannibalism. When the captives lived in England, they told detailed stories about people-eating orgies, and these were believed and became widespread. Fitzroy thought them cannibals, and Darwin believed the same. The latter recorded that the captain of a sealing vessel was told by a Fuegian "boy" that his people suffocated old women in the smoke from fires and then ate them, and Jemmy told similar stories. There is no factual evidence, however, that the Fuegians resorted to cannibalism for feasting or even during famines. Such descriptions were pure fabrications told apparently to fascinate the English.

Darwin's book about his five-year trip around the world, titled *The Voyage of the Beagle*, appeared first in 1839 and was such an immediate success that it was reprinted twice within the first year. The book is a natural history in diary form and contains information not only about the Fuegians but about other tribal people as well. It was such books, although this is a rather recent example compared with many others, that offered a broad audience of readers firsthand descriptions of non-Europeans who were primitive. As readable as Darwin's descriptions of peoples are, none present the subjects in depth. It is rather remarkable and most notable that the first reasonably well-rounded ethnography written about any tribal people appeared in 1851 and was about the Iroquois Indians of New York state. The study was authored by Lewis Henry Morgan (1818–1881), a lawyer who subsequently became famous as an anthropologist. At about this time and even earlier, other books describing nonliterate peoples appeared, but none were as broadly based as Morgan's *League of the Iroquois*. Europeans and Americans who read books with a competent interpretation of nonliterates began to realize that all peoples around the world shared similar, basic problems of survival, and that men differed only in the ways in which their needs were satisfied.

At this point when time, space, and cultural relativity began to coalesce, it was possible for anthropologists and their idea of culture to appear. With the expanded knowledge of earthly time and space and with its accurate measurement, Euro-Americans could become familiar with the diverse peoples of the world and could begin seeking new answers to the questions of man's age on earth and the diversity of his ways.

3

MAN'S BIOLOGICAL EMERGENCE

One of the most remarkable observations about human life is that the germ plasm in each of us represents the unbroken chain of life itself. In the recent geological past, somewhat more than two million years ago, this plasm was present in creatures from whom men soon would evolve. To discuss this era when the physical qualities characteristic of men were beginning to emerge should help satisfy the intellectual curiosity in most of us about our distant ancestors. The ideas of "descent from apes" and of "missing links" have an intriguing appeal which invites investigation. This discussion furthermore serves as a prelude for introducing the modern races of men.

In the past few years so much new and reasonably precise information about man's physical emergence has been discovered that if this trend continues, the interpretations of today probably will not stand intact for very long. My purpose nonetheless is to utilize the data currently available in order to probe remote time and space along the bony trail that leads to modern man. The presentation of such information about man's emergence offers an opportunity to comprehend how we came to be our particular biological type.

Although it may not seem profound, it is pertinent to note that people, like chickens, walk on two legs, and women, like shrews, give birth to live young. Men and women, like seals, have large brains in proportion to their body weights, but unlike most turtles, human males have an external appearance which is different from that of the females. These observations emphasize that we share with many vertebrates diverse and complex biological characteristics, and yet our species, like any other, is defined on the basis of its unique structural combinations. One of man's most critical anatomical combinations is that of his limbs with the shoulder or hip joints; this arrangement makes possible our freely swinging arms as well as our upright stance and walking motions. The feet on which a human stands are important, but their significance is minor compared with that of his hands. Human wrist and finger movements, plus thumbs which are opposable, comprise a highly versatile combination. Man's ability to coordinate thumb and finger movements to perform delicate tasks as well as powerful feats is awe-inspiring and uniquely human. As a result of our upright posture, our heads reach high, and we are also famous for our oversized brains. When the configuration of bones in the skull and the tooth pattern are added to the other characteristics cited, we have the basic structural components of our species, *Homo sapiens*, man the wise, the intelligent, or as some would prefer, the "wise guy." We were named scientifically in 1758 by Carolus Linnaeus (1707–1778). Although it has become necessary to separate some of the plant and animal species designated by Linnaeus, no revision from the 1758 classification is necessary for man. A species is a series of regional populations in which members of any one population are able to breed with those of any other even though there may be limited differences in external appearance and genetic composition. So it is with all men, no matter where they may live on this earth.

THE AFRICAN ADAM In 1871, Charles Darwin postulated that our immediate precursors would most likely be found in Africa. The presence there of man's remote but living relatives, the gorilla and chimpanzee, led him to reason that somewhere on the same continent was man's evolutionary Eden. Darwin's prediction did not begin to bear fruit until 1924, but since that time the major discoveries pertaining to human evolution have been made in Africa. The first critical discovery, made in 1924, was near Taung in Rhodesia. Here the skull of a primate about six years of age at the time of its death was obtained by Raymond A. Dart. The specimen came to be called *Australopithecus africanus*, or southern ape from Africa. It is convenient and justifiable to term this fossil, and the others subsequently recovered which are similar, as the "Southern Man-Apes." The braincase of this primeval child is small, in profile the lower face protrudes, and the jaw is chinless. After the initial find, the remains of mature Southern Man-Apes were discovered, and these reveal much more about the species. In general terms, they are comparatively large brained, with cranial capacities ranging from 450 to 600 cubic centimeters as compared with a mean of 1500 cc for modern man, some 500 cc for a gorilla, or 400 for a chimpanzee. Brain size, however, is at present useful only as a broadly comparative statistic. More significant is the fact that the fossils involved have occipital condyles, or projections on the base of the skull surface to which the vertebrae attach. Since these are located in nearly the same anatomical position as those of modern man, an upright posture seems likely. Added evidence for their upstanding pose and accompanying bipedal gait is the fact that their pelvic bones do not differ in any remarkable manner from those of modern man. The general structure of the bones suggests that the Southern Man-Apes were small creatures, weighing up to about ninety pounds, and that although their heads looked ape-like, their limbs and bodies were similar to modern man's in form.

In Tanzania at a deeply eroded gorge called Olduvai an important discovery of fossil bones was made in 1960 by L. B. S. Leakey. One cluster included part of a mandible, portions of a skull, some hand bones, and a few teeth; all of these appear to have belonged to a young individual. At four other sites in the same general area, bones and teeth which are morphologically similar to those of the juvenile were recovered; collectively they have been classified by some as fossils of a true man termed *Homo habilis*, or more euphemistically, as "Handy Man" since the word "habilis" translates as "able, skilled, or handy." In two sites containing his bones are stone tools which he probably made. How long ago these bones and tools belonged to living peoples is not clear, but possibly the time was more than a million and a half years ago. In one of these very ancient sites stone tools and some bones of Handy Man were found with the bones of a Southern Man-Ape.

The relationship between the Southern Man-Ape and Handy Man is contested at present. Some paleoanthropologists stoutly maintain that the two are at least second cousins, whereas others argue with equal conviction that they are not even kissing cousins. One argument to support the disparity between the Southern Man-Ape and Handy Man is that the former had a cranial capacity of from 450 to 600 cc, whereas Handy Man's brains had filled out to around 680 cc. Thus, the latter may have had superior intellectual capabilities, but all of this disagreement may be an unimportant splitting of cubic centimeters. In any case, in the few deposits which contain the bones of

Southern Man-Apes and no Handy Man bones, stone tools are not found. Thus, these Southern Man-Apes were not clearly stone-knappers, although some of their number elsewhere did make bone tools and utilize natural bones as tools. Thus there is evidence of some cultural behavior for both forms, and both had comparatively large brains, upright posture, and hands that, although probably less versatile than those of modern man, were nonetheless capable of efficient manipulation. My inclination is to lump the two and to call them African Man-Apes. The word "man" precedes "ape" because both types had culture, but the word "ape" is retained to indicate that anatomically these beings were only half a step removed from their ape contemporaries. If any evidence currently available represents a missing link, it is these finds.

LADDERS, CHAINS, AND LINKS   A "ladder" gave way to a "chain" whose "links" came to represent evolution. This sentence obviously begs for clarification. The "Ladder of Nature" was the way in which Aristotle (384–322 B.C.) ordered life. The various rungs represented levels of complexity in earthly forms. At the bottom were inorganic forms, next vegetables, and then animals. Aristotle believed that although individual organisms had only a transient existence, their species were permanent and, being fixed in form, could be ranked. In his view each of these natural levels was static, with no advancement from one to another. Aristotle's "Ladder of Nature" was interpreted in allegorical and religious terms by medieval Europeans. The ladder was considered to represent a series of contiguous but discrete creations, with the least complex forms interpreted as being literally low, physically simple, and spiritually inferior, whereas the most complex forms were literally high, physically complex, and spiritually superior. God was thought to command this hierarchy from his celestial home, with man standing upright and taller than almost any other animal as he reached for heavenly climes. The ladder gradually came to be viewed more as a linked continuum or vertical chain, with each form or link possessing the divine right to kill or dominate all of those which were lower on the scale. In the seventeenth and eighteenth centuries God's position as a commander shifted to that of engineer or designer, and the "Great Chain of Being" was viewed in a new perspective. The emphasis here was on the gradation of forms, with a recognition that only minute differences separated species from their nearest neighbors. This was now thought to represent the grand design of God to bring almost perfect order into the universe. Again, however, there was no idea that one form had mutated into another; all were considered fixed in the image of their original creation. Two critical links appeared to be missing from this Great Chain of Being. The first of these was between man and apes. Great apes clearly were quite similar to man in physical form, but they were mute linguistically and were without culture. This difference seemed too great to represent the simple gradation from one link to another, and therefore it seemed that another link must belong between the two. The second link missing was thought to be one between man and God. It was felt that when knowledge of this and other worlds became more complete, it might be found that the latter gap actually represented the level of angels, superior incorporeal beings, or supermen existing in other worlds.

Although we are still unable to supply a link between God and man, the link between apes and men is now reasonably well filled by the African Man-Apes. At the time they lived other ape-forms also inhabited Africa, but because these others refused to stay out of trees, their progeny became the gorillas or chimpanzees of today. To say that man descended from apes is in a sense true, for the ancestor of the man-apes did resemble the apes of today more than modern man. If one wishes to think in these terms, it would be more reasonable to homogenize a modern gorilla, chimpanzee, and man, thereby negating their specialized characteristics which have developed over the past two million years, and say that the resultant being is the same as the ancestor of all three and thus represents the missing link.

The search for a pattern in the forms of animals clearly was pre-Darwinian. However, it was not until after Darwin published *Origin of Species* in 1859 that the idea of changes leading one species to develop into another became an acceptable working hypothesis. Furthermore, it was not until early in the present century, with a rediscovery and expansion of the genetic studies by Gregor Mendel (1822–1884), that the particularistic nature of the evolutionary process became broadly understood and could be accepted. By the time the first African Man-Ape remains were reported in 1924, the nature of biological evolution already had been established firmly.

MODERN MAN One of the historically early finds of fossil man was made in central Java by the Dutch anatomist Eugene Dubois. In 1891 he discovered the upper portion of a skull and some teeth; the following year he uncovered a thighbone or femur. This combination of teeth and bones was called Java Man (originally *Pithecanthropus* *erectus,* but now *Homo erectus erectus*), and remains of seven other individuals with the same general characteristics were recovered in Java by 1939. Java Man, who lived about 700,000 years ago, was a little-big-head with a cranial capacity ranging from 775 to 975 cc. Originally, Java Man was labeled an "ape man," but he recently has been elevated taxonomically to the status of a "man." He well might have been granted this position earlier if it were certain that he manufactured tools. One critical means of distinguishing man from all other animals is man's tool-making ability. Direct evidence for the use of tools by Java Man has not been found as yet, but it is now known that his close relative who lived in China, called Peking Man (formerly *Sinanthropus pekinensis* but now *Homo erectus pekinensis*), manufactured tools. Between 1923 and 1937 in the caves near the town of Choukoutien the bones and teeth of at least forty Peking persons were found. They lived from 300,000 to 600,000 years ago and used fire from their earliest days. The chipped stone tools found among their bones were crude and varied but were clearly man-made products.

The human bones from China and Java are not really very old if one considers the total course of man's genealogical evolution. If we could magically cover these bones with flesh and clothes and have our creations walk along the sidewalk of a busy city, they probably would attract no more attention than a battered professional fighter or a beetle-browed army general. The skulls of these far easterners differ somewhat from those of modern men, but below the head their bodies vary from modern man only in rather trivial morphological details. These bones represent the next to the last link in the human chain culminating in modern man.

In terms of physical evolution the Southern Man-Ape appears to have been more ape-like than Handy Man, if in fact a difference separated the two, but more importantly both evidenced cultural behavior. By the time of Peking Man, however, the equation of human bones with cultural evidence is indisputable. In general, the Peking population probably emerged from a Handy Man form. The skull of Peking Man still differed somewhat from that of modern man; his brain was smaller, skull thicker, brows more pronounced, and teeth larger. Finds which were much the same as Java and Peking man *(Homo erectus)* include jaws and a skull fragment from Terifine, Algeria; a face and jaw from Swartkrans, South Africa; a skull bone from Vertesszollos, Hungary; and a skull from a level above the Handy Man associations at Olduvai. Modern man emerged as a clearly distinct creature about 500,000 years ago and is best represented by finds in Europe. The Steinheim skull from Germany, the two Fontechevade skulls from France, and skull fragments from Swanscombe in England all represent men in the modern sense.

SPECIES AND RACES It has been noted already that all living men belong to a single species, *Homo sapiens,* and that our species designation has required no revision since it was set forth in 1758. A species, according to one definition, is composed of actually or potentially inbreeding populations which are reproductively isolated from other groups. In other words, the members of a single species inbreed or are fully capable of inbreeding and are isolated from the individuals in another species in terms of reproductive capacity rather than in terms of geography. In the context of humans, a Negro in the southeastern United States does not breed with a Caucasian because social ideals separate them, but if such a mating occurred, a fertile offspring could be produced. Another deterrent to breeding between peoples of different races is geographical separation. Distance prevents an Eskimo from mating with a Bantu of South Africa, but if this geographical factor were eliminated, the Eskimo and Bantu would be able to mate and produce fertile offspring. Thus all races of men are members of one species, and together they form a closed breeding system.

Although the definition of a species is clear-cut and straightforward, that of race is not. It seems to me that race most often is defined in one of four distinct ways, depending on the background of the individual using the term.

1. "A race is a group of people with a similar sociocultural background and/or a similar stereotypic appearance." It is within the context of a definition such as this that some people speak of a "Jewish," "French," or "English" race. With respect to the Jews the stress is sociocultural and religious, although there is in addition a physical stereotype. The French and English "races" are considered distinct on the basis of national identities which are broadly sociocultural. When the emphasis is primarily on physical appearance, types such as the "Negro" or "Nordic" may be isolated. Although some of the "races" arising from this definition coincide with those proposed by anthropologists, others do not. This definition is inadequate because it does not base distinctions on consistent criteria, and yet it has a certain "common sense" appeal which makes it difficult to refute in simple terms. Because of its arbitrary base, it is likely to be the cause of various ethnocentric biases and distortions.

2. "Races are breeding stocks, among which there are superior and inferior potentialities." This definition of race probably would be acceptable to most racists. The implication is that human breeding isolates exist and not only have distinct physical characteristics but possess differential intellectual capacities and unlike potentialities for achievement. These terms are used by racists to categorize superior and inferior races. The Negro race is considered by some whites as the prime example of an inferior group, and these same whites consider themselves to be the standard bearers of achievement and civilization. Furthermore, the supporters of this view hold that race mixture produces individuals with qualities which are inferior to those of either of the races involved in the mating. There is nothing hazy or unclear in this point of view, but neither is there any positive evidence to support it.

3. "A race is a human population which has inbred to the point that it exhibits a distinctive configuration of physical characteristics." Here the emphasis is on human morphology and on such external manifestations of it as head shape, skin color, hair texture, and the configuration of facial features. This is the anatomical view of race which has been supported by most physical anthropologists. On this basis J. F. Blumenbach, in 1775, distinguished five races: American or red, Ethiopian or black, Caucasian or white, Malayan or brown, and Mongolian or yellow. One major difficulty in the morphological definition of race is that one race blends into another in areas where any of them meet, creating mixtures which are difficult to categorize. This has led to refinements of the classification, which in one system results in nine races and in another includes twenty-nine races and subraces. If subdividing such as this continues, there is seemingly no end to the number of possible categories, and this would make the anatomical concept of race operationally and conceptually difficult. Furthermore, and of more importance, the classifiers do not agree about the positions of particular populations, which means that there are nearly as many different racial taxonomies as there are different taxonomists. Finally, very little is known about the heritability of anatomical characteristics, and this is perhaps the most telling criticism of the concept.

4. "A race is a population that differs in the presence or frequency of certain genes." Here the definition is not based on gross anatomical or broadly conceived cultural characteristics. It is not grounded in emotional feelings, nor in an infinitely wide variety of combinations of particular morphological characteristics. Instead, the genetic definition is based on the particularistic transmission of biological quali-

ties. This definition recognizes only the importance of genotypes and the perpetuation of specific characteristics, and its usage requires precise knowledge of the genes which determine particular characteristics. Thus it is distinctly limited in its present applicability since we know very little yet about the precise genetic attributes of most inherited characteristics. Currently it is blood-group genes, in terms of their frequencies, which offer the greatest potential for distinguishing one people from another. It is impossible to give a ready classification of races of mankind within a genetic framework at present, since in these terms a race is still largely a statistical cluster of individuals who differ from other clusters in terms of specific gene frequencies.

As a species is a closed genetic system, races are open genetic systems, meaning that genes may be exchanged among the members of different races. The characteristics of a race tend to be unstable since such genetic exchanges do occur and probably have been occurring during most of human time. Thus, there arise combinations and recombinations of characteristics which are not likely to be stable for any length of time. A realization of this lack of physical constancy has led some physical anthropologists to abandon the concept of race. The same anthropologists feel too that the emotional attachments which surround the word "race" make the term of limited scientific value. They conclude that since the genetic concept of population differences is the only reasonable one, and since it is only a statistical concept, groups of people differ from one another only in relative terms with reference to gene frequencies. Another alternative to replace the idea of race has been suggested; it is to classify populations as "ethnic groups." Such a group would be defined as a human population which has developed physical and sociocultural differences because of isolating mechanisms which are social or geographic.

One question which must be raised concerns the origins of the distinctive physical appearance of widely separated populations. It has been argued by some that the ancestral stock of man began to diversify physically long ago and that the major racial divisions have largely independent histories. Others argue that the present racial distinctions arose in the very recent past. If we admit the probability of gene exchanges among diverse populations through most of human time, we must assume that such intermingling precludes the possibility of distinct physical differences remaining unchanged over a long time period. At present most physical anthropologists favor the hypothesis that a single human ancestral stock gave rise to modern man and that the racial diversity which we see today is comparatively recent in its emergence. In any event, all would agree that the major factor which has produced the regional variations in human appearances is natural selection operating on mutations within populations having a certain degree of physical isolation.

A mutation is a permanent and abrupt change in the character of a particular gene. Mutations may serve as the basis for lasting genetic changes in a population, but the mutations alone are not enough. A mutation creates a new genetic characteristic in an organism, and this change may or may not be advantageous in the particular setting in which the mutant form finds itself. It is at this point that natural selection enters, and the environment in which the organism exists becomes critical. If a particular mutant has qualities advantageous within the environment, it is likely to be perpetuated more successfully than other forms in which the mutation has not taken place. Thus, natural selection is based on the interplay between the environment and the mutant or nonmutant forms. Assuming that the environment remains constant, the form with the greater survival potential will begin to replace the other. It should be realized that because the nonmutants already are adapted to the environment, any mutant's advantage or disadvantage over the nonmutant will only be slight. A shift in the environment may change the balance at any time; such a shift gives selective advantages to the nonmutant rather than to the mutant.

In these terms, "survival of the fittest" emerges as a functional concept in genetic terms only, and involves no deliberate volition on the part of the organism. For example, within a particular environment natural selection undoubtedly has favored mutant genes which produced human populations with different skin colors. Although the precise genetic factors producing different skin pigmentations remain unknown, it can be said that skin color in man has been adaptive for different environments. Dark-skinned populations developed in geographical areas having high temperatures, a great deal of sunlight, and high humidity, whereas lightly pigmented peoples predominate in areas with contrasting environmental factors. It would appear that these differences in skin colors have survival advantages in specific settings and arose from particular genes which mutated and subsequently dominated because of natural selectivity. Because peoples with slightly different genetic patterns have interbred for most of human time, innumerable groups of people give the appearance of being "blends" or "mixtures" of the major racial stocks. However, no race is intrinsically "pure," and there is a constant overlap in genetic characteristics from one population to another which clearly unites all of mankind.

HUMAN RACES: A GENERAL STATEMENT The contemporary scientific view about the nature of human racial variations may best be summarized in terms of the 1952 "Statement on the Nature of Race and Race Differences" prepared by physical anthropologists and geneticists under United Nations sponsorship. The eight descriptive points contained in the statement are summarized and discussed below.

1. "Scientists are generally agreed that all men living today belong to a single species, *Homo sapiens*, and are derived from a common stock, even though there is some dispute as to when and how different human groups diverged from this common stock." In these terms the concept of race is viewed as a taxonomic means to facilitate studies of human populations. The statement indicates that of all human groups found in the past, only *Homo sapiens* survived to the present. All men living today must necessarily belong to this species, and any physical differences serve only as a means of distinguishing the variability within the species.

2. "Some of the physical differences between human groups are due to differences in hereditary constitution and some to differences in the environments in which they have been brought up." Thus, the genetic and environmental factors contributing to an individual's biological nature must be weighed in combination. The isolation of populations from one another, mutations, and natural selection give rise to inheritable characteristics which have differential environmental survival value. Heredity and environment combine to form the basis of physical differences which, although seemingly pronounced, probably have become distinct only recently in human history.

3. "National, religious, geographical, linguistic and cultural groups do not necessarily coincide with racial groups; and the cultural traits of such groups have no demonstrated connexion with racial traits." Thus, race, language, and culture do not form an inseparable triumvirate but are much more likely to vary independently of one another.

4. "Human races can be, and have been, classified in different ways by different anthropologists. Most of them agree in classifying the greater part of existing mankind into at least three large units, which may be called major groups. . . ." The classification is based on a configuration of physical characteristics, and there is no evidence for either the superiority or inferiority of any particular group or race.

5. "Most anthropologists do not include mental characteristics in

their classification of human races. Studies within a single race have shown that both innate capacity and environmental opportunity determine the results of tests of intelligence and temperament, though their relative importance is disputed." Experience with intelligence tests suggests that persons of one race perform at the same level as those of another if they are from like environmental backgrounds. There is no evidence to suggest that racial classification can be made on the basis of intellectual capacity.

6. "The scientific material available to us at present does not justify the conclusion that inherited genetic differences are a major factor in producing the differences between the cultures and cultural achievements of different peoples or groups." In fact, just the opposite appears to be true. The physical environment appears to have more important effects on cultural developments than does any other factor.

7. "There is no evidence for the existence of so-called 'pure' races." Mixture of human groups has been taking place for a long, but not a clearly established, span of time.

8. "We now have to consider the bearing of these statements on the problem of human equality. We wish to emphasize that equality of opportunity and equality in law in no way depend, as ethical principles, upon the assertion that human beings are in fact equal in endowment." The statement on race sponsored by the United Nations concludes with a summary to the effect that the differences among races are physical in nature and that the intellectual and emotional capacities among the races are not innately different. It further states that sociocultural changes in man's ways are not linked to changes in racial types and that from a biological perspective there is nothing disadvantageous in racial mixtures.

As a conclusion to this discussion about attitudes toward race, it is enlightening to consider the matter briefly as it has emerged among ourselves in the recent past. By assuming a historical perspective we should come to better understand the basis of our thoughts. By the mid-nineteenth century most persons were convinced that there was no equality among the races of man. This attitude, shared by most tribal and folk societies, became formalized in "scientific racism," to explain behavioral differences among peoples. It was proposed by some that the nonwhite races had "degenerated" and by others that there had been multiple creations for the races, with Caucasians endowed with superior intelligence. Admittedly, contrary views also existed, and one of these maintained that differences among men reflected adaptations to contrasting environments. The discovery of nonwhites around the world soon was followed by an extended era of colonialism. The enslavement of some peoples and the gross economic exploitation of others were justified on the basis of different inherent capabilities among the races. It was not until the early part of the present century that some persons, anthropologists included, came to realize that racism had no scientific validity and that it thrived primarily as a major justification for the suppression of less complex peoples. Quite clearly, racism is not yet dead among ourselves, and it should be noted that it thrives best in those areas of this country and the world where the economic exploitation of nonwhites is favored.

4

BECOMING HUMAN

In the beginning there were creatures who became men because they developed cultural behavior. Culture is the handiwork of man alone, and its first recognized bearers were the African Man-Apes. One may subscribe to the thesis that a superior deity created man from a void of nothingness, but this viewpoint has limited acceptance today. If one assumes an evolutionary perspective, it must be acknowledged that man developed from some previously existing animal. Within recent years the case for man's place in evolution has begun to emerge with considerable clarity. The common ancestor of modern men and apes appears to have lived in Africa about ten million years ago during the late Miocene or early Pliocene. Contemporary apes and men share affinities in their shoulder and arm morphology, in their dental pattern, and in other anatomical characteristics. In other highly specific details the African apes, the gorilla and chimpanzee, are more similar to man than are the Asiatic species of apes. The number of chromosomes and their form virtually are identical in the chimpanzee and man; African apes and man have the same types of serum protein, primate hemoglobin, serum albumin, and gamma globulin. They also are hosts to many of the same types of internal parasites. This list of particular similarities between African apes and man may be contrasted with comparisons between man and all other mammalian forms to clearly demonstrate our close genetic affinity with apes. It is irrefutable that men evolved from a form of ape.

If, as is presumed, man, chimpanzees, and gorillas share a common ancestor who lived over eight million years ago, we may expect one or both of these apes to exhibit behavior which is broadly reflective of human behavior. The modern gorilla, because of its very specialized physical characteristics developed in adaptation to the narrow but bountiful ecological niche which it occupies, is less similar to humans than is the chimpanzee. Anatomically as well as in terms of the characteristics cited above, the chimpanzee is the primate most similar to man. Furthermore, chimpanzees live in an ecological setting which, because of seasonal scarcities of edible products, requires a flexibility of food-getting practices which more nearly approaches conditions among men than among gorillas. The observations of wild chimpanzees suggest that they are more likely to pick up various objects when searching for food than at any other time. The tools that these apes use are also more varied than those reported for any other animal except man. For example, the chimpanzees in the Gombe Stream Reserve in Tanzania habitually prepare sticks which they use to probe ant or termite holes. The insects grasp the twig, are removed from their hole while clinging to the twig, and are then eaten. When water is so scarce that just a little remains in tree boles, the chimpanzees gather leaves, chew them slightly, press them together, and dip the wad into a bole to soak up the water. After retrieving the wet leaves, they suck the water from the bundle. Leaves also serve to remove dirt, sticky substances, and water from their hands and bodies. In addition, a chimpanzee may pick up and throw any object at a potential enemy in order to delay its pursuit. Most importantly, it appears that these behavior patterns are learned by the young from adults. Clearly, chimpanzees possess a flexibility in thinking, learning behavior, and tool-using ability. Since these qualities must have been important dimensions in the earliest human life, here again is collateral evidence of the ape-man relationship.

THE FIRST MEN The African Man-Apes are the earliest known tool-makers, and because of this they are the first mammals to be classified as men. These individuals lived at least two million years ago, and their bones have been recovered most commonly in southern and eastern Africa. The cultural evidence is clearest at sites in the vicinity of Olduvai Gorge, which was then a semiarid parkland setting. Living here on a mud surface near a lake, the African Man-Apes hunted

and brought in pebbles from elsewhere to use in their natural condition or to fashion into implements. If a thin pebble was to be modified
purposefully, it was struck at one edge with another stone to remove
one or two flakes. Flakes were detached from both faces if it was a
thick pebble. Such stones, purposefully fractured, are called Oldowan
split pebbles (Figure 6), and the pebbles as well as the flakes struck

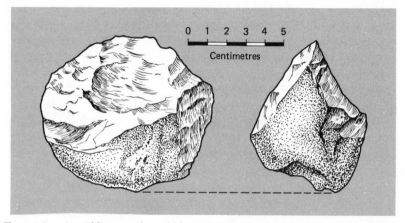

Figure 6.   *An Oldowan split pebble tool (Courtesy of L. B. S. Leaky, Olduvai
Gorge, Cambridge University Press, 1951).*

from them probably were used as cutting tools. The production of
these simple stone artifacts represents an accomplishment of far
greater importance than the first casting of iron or the first splitting
of the atom. The development of stoneworking abilities was the base
from which most subsequent technological achievements emerged.
The earliest evidence that individuals took a form from nature and
then modified it to better suit their purposes is at Olduvai Gorge.
We will never know how ape-men came to produce the first split-
pebble artifact, and yet we might assume that it was not by preconceived plan. I conjecture that some dull-toothed female was pounding
a piece of meat with a pebble in order to make her meal more easily
chewable, and that when her attention was diverted momentarily, the
pebble struck another pounding stone on the ground nearby and
fractured. Rather than stop to find a new pebble, she continued to use
the broken one, and soon she realized that it did more than just break
down the fibers of the meat. The sharp stone was actually cutting it
into pieces far better than her worn teeth would be able to. In these
terms the first cutting implement served as a substitute for human

teeth, and the discovery of its potential was accidental. Although this creation was unintentional, the point vital for the future is that the individual involved had the intelligence to realize what she had accomplished. The second essential point is that the idea was remembered and the original action later repeated, but this time with preconceived purpose. In other words, the utility of such a cutting tool was realized as soon as it had been created fortuitously. The advantage of the Oldowan split pebble no doubt was apparent first to older persons with worn teeth, and then it came to be copied or shared by all as a cutting device more efficient than even the sharpest teeth of a youth. From this humble beginning the cumulative patterning of culture now began to emerge, and it would be a matter of only a little less than two million years before bingo and the bomb became an intimate part of culture.

How the first Oldowan pebble tool came into existence must remain conjectural, but it may be reasonably suggested that prehumans had used natural tools long before they learned to make tools. Modern ape and monkey behavior is tangentially helpful when discussing the transition to man. Both wild apes and monkeys handle or throw objects during displays of aggression, and they handle objects even more during food-getting efforts. If we combine the two activities and add a biological potential for efficient manipulation of objects, we have isolated at least two important factors which would lead man to develop greater food procurement efficiency than could be realized by apes. After learning to obtain food in this way, the ape-man applied his skill to pick up a rock during an aggressive display, throw it, and kill his foe. As stones came to be so aimed and then thrown, a greater potential for survival was achieved and the first use of an effective weapon became established.

At this point it must be interjected that the transition from apemen to man-apes required a long span of time, probably millions of years. Possibly the transitional ape-men who made the shift from tool-using to actual tool production were rather like modern chimpanzees. By the time the earliest African Man-Apes had become distinctive, they were bipedal and had a flexibility of finger and thumb movements. Also of importance, their canine teeth were relatively small in contrast to their large molars. These dental characteristics indicate that canine teeth had not been utilized to tear the flesh of other animals for many generations and that broad-crowned molars were developed in response to the abrasive nature of the foods consumed. It is reasonable to suggest that stones already had replaced teeth as the important weapons or tools. A stone used in the hand or accurately thrown was in a sense an extension of the function of teeth or fists as weapons, whereas the split Oldowan pebbles used for cutting were substitutes for teeth as tools.

After tool production had been achieved by one individual and the idea conveyed to others who imitated the process, we find that APE-men had developed into the status of MAN-apes. The critical components of culture are its learned and shared dimensions, and because of the similarities among the split pebbles recovered, culture clearly is in evidence. In addition to the implications of their stone-working, it is possible to make a few additional inferences concerning these man-apes. The concentrations of worked and unworked stones found with animal bones indicate that these people were at least part-time hunters. The bones are from diverse species, but only portions of larger animals are represented. This suggests that the hunters killed their game elsewhere and carried as much as they could to particular spots at which they and others could eat. Many of the bones are from small species such as frogs and lizards or from young animals of larger species. The scarcity of bones from larger animals suggests that these man-apes did not routinely kill large animals. The clusters of split pebbles and broken bones probably represent the temporary camps of several families who roamed together about the countryside. As populations increased and as local food or material resources were depleted, men roamed to the borders of areas they habitually exploited and then pushed on into unknown territories. Their descendants continued to follow the same basic pattern for at least a million years. The only change was that the way of life spread farther, including most of Africa as well as reaching into southern Europe and into Asia. The descendants of the African Man-Apes were able to expand their geographical range because they had applied their mental abilities to develop an increasingly useful tool—culture—which enabled them to adapt to more varied environments.

The reader probably realizes that I have not been precise in establishing the nature of the relationship between the Southern Man-Apes and Handy Man. I have grouped them as African Man-Apes for most purposes but acknowledge that this arrangement may not be correct. The problem is that both creatures had reached the level of being human since both possessed culture, and yet the cultural evidence for the Southern Man-Apes is not as clear and neat as for Handy Man. In caves along with the bones of one form of Southern Man-Ape were the bones of animals he killed and ate. Prominent among his kills were baboons, whose skulls often were crushed on the left side at the front. Many such shattered baboon skulls have marks which suggest that the blow was delivered with a double-edged implement. In these caves were a disproportionate number of antelope femurs which, with their double condyle on one end, well might have served as baboon-killing clubs. From the large proportion of antelope jaws, with one half detached from the other, it would seem that they too were used as weapons or tools. Since these bones were not artificially changed by man-apes, they are not quite artifacts. Finds associated with australopithecines from Makapansgat, South Africa, include sections of broken bones with one stuck inside another as well as long slivers of fractured bones, another indication of a bone-working industry of a cultural nature.

Out of the expanded base of Oldowan stoneworking another lithic complex, termed Chellean-Acheulean, emerged in Africa; it declined only about 60,000 years ago. In its first stage it was characterized by the split pebbles as well as by natural stones used as hammers or bashers. In the second level the hand ax clearly is the most diagnostic or distinctive, even if not the most prevalent, stone tool. The earliest hand axes were natural stones from which a number of flakes had been removed to produce a sharp point at one end (Figure 7). These all-purpose tools served to chop meat and sinew, skin an animal, or

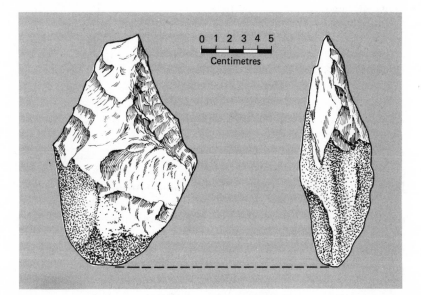

Figure 7. An early form of hand ax (Courtesy of L. B. S. Leaky, Olduvai Gorge, Cambridge University Press, 1951).

break bones to retrieve the marrow. As time passed, the flakes were detached from hand-ax cores with greater precision and regularity, an indication of improved human coordination in working stone. At this stage, termed Chellean, in the Olduvai Gorge country men cooperated in herding game animals onto soft, marshy ground where they might be stoned to death. The hunters made their hand axes at these sites in order to butcher the slain animals at once. Found in the next period in time, Acheulean, at Terifine in North Africa are the bones of *Homo erectus*, and he too obtained his food by killing animals bogged down along lake shores. Here again the general pattern of living in Africa drew men to lakes, rivers, and springs, but they did not comfortably range into forests or over grasslands. By the end of this period the tool tradition had become much the same over the inhabited world. People lived primarily in Africa, although some occupied the area from western Europe to southern India. Drawing evidence from various sites we may suggest that windbreaks were man's earliest nonnatural shelters. The few wooden artifacts known include clubs and sticks thought to have been used as digging sticks or possibly as spears. In stone a great proliferation of forms took place; these ranged from heavy mattocks to a wide variety of knives. At this time, too, family members no doubt sat around campfires at night and talked with one another.

FIRE AND MAN   Of all man's accomplishments it is impossible to single out one as the culmination, but unerringly we know that among the most important was his learning to control fire. Although fire was not used by man until comparatively late in Africa, it was utilized in China about 600,000 years ago. In Europe fire was used by cave dwellers in the Durance River valley of southern France some 750,000 years ago. Here the evidence is clear, for in one cave are bits of charcoal, ashes, fire-cracked stones, and hearths up to a yard in diameter. Man must have acquired fire considerably earlier since in the Durance cave he clearly had it under firm control.

A virtual magic envelops the leaping flames of fire, and its existence has long served as an inviting topic for both oral and written literature. Fire may be feared, respected, or worshipped, but above all else it must be controlled. With a reasonable degree of confidence we may speculate about how man first became familiar with fire. Fire from natural causes most often results when lightning strikes forest trees, although natural fires also are associated with live volcanoes and coal deposits lighted spontaneously. A raging fire swept out of control by winds is terrifying to primitives and modern man alike, but a small fire burning quietly is arresting and compelling in its attraction. Man and many other animals, even fish, may gaze spellbound at a fire. To play with fire is to court at least a slight burn, and yet it was probably by toying with a small fire that man first began to realize its potential usefulness.

One of the first associations usually drawn between fire and man is that of the flames and coals of a campfire providing warmth. Without a protective coat of natural fur, early man could effectively occupy only tropical, arid, and mild temperate areas. The geographical range of nude men might be extended somewhat through natural selection which resulted in cold-resistant populations, but even given such a biological advantage, the effective range of such a people was extremely limited. However, with fire to offer artificial warmth, especially during the chill of night, men without clothing could travel as far as the margins of cold, alien environments with moderate success. After men controlled fire, they could range into areas where no one had gone before and reap rich harvests of game in these virgin lands. Before such extensions abroad could be successful, it was necessary to transport fire as burning embers from one camp to the next. Fire may have been carried by children, as it is among some modern primitives who do not know how to produce it artificially. At the beginning of man's use of fire there is no reason to think that he created it; he only borrowed it from nature and artificially extended its life. Once men customarily blew glowing embers into flames and made campfires at the end of the day, they were able to modify their own futures. Before the use of campfires, man must have settled down for the night at dusk and fallen to sleep soon thereafter. His rest would be fretful, however, since an individual who slept soundly on the ground while marauding carnivores were about might not be alive in the morning. It is possible that until fire was controlled and effective weapons were developed, men slept in trees as do most modern apes and monkeys. After learning to build fires, campers could rest more securely because predators would not approach flames closely even though the promise of a meal was nearby.

The rhythm of life, with day as the time for subsistence activities and night as the time to sleep, changed with the acquisition of fire. In a sense, day was extended with the light of campfires but not to the point that it was possible to duplicate daytime behavior at night. Firelight lengthened the day only within a narrow, flickering circle, and yet it is not difficult to imagine this setting as leading to a revolution in human behavior. As children fell asleep near the fire, adults remained awake to talk about the day's events, to consider what might be done on the day to follow, to make or repair implements, but most of all perhaps to think in a new, abstract way. Although immediate problems of survival could be handled effectively only during daylight hours, the time before drowsiness could be devoted to new thought processes, to musing and to meditation. It was around such fires, too, as men stared into the flames and took comfort in the radiating warmth, that stories became myths and world views became crystallized as philosophies.

As fire became a stabilized part of his culture, an even more fundamental change took place in man himself. Before fire the physiological clock in man was linked with the sun's movements and regulated his life; his daily cycle had been geared to twelve hours of activity and twelve hours of rest. After fire had extended the twelve hours of day, he eventually broke his natural cycle and lengthened his hours of activity. This led not only to the late show but to the late, late show.

As more time passed, man improved his abilities to utilize fire, and it came to serve many diverse purposes. It was no doubt used as a hunting aid and to drive frightened animals from caves so that men could take their place; with a nightly fire at the entrance, such a shelter became a snug and relatively secure home. The use of fire to cook food was another important change. Since cooked meat preserves longer than raw meat, it now was possible to accumulate temporary surpluses. Another advantage of cooked meat was that it could be chewed and digested more readily.

If you pause for a moment and consider all the things that you accomplish after the sun has set, your thanks should go back nearly a million years when, with fire, the change toward night-living began in man. When you stare into a fire and are transfixed by the configuration of flames with their almost sensual warmth, you may not have realized that you are expressing an old, old human feeling of awe and security that began when the first hearths created the first real homes for men.

FAMILY LIFE BEGINS As a hearth symbolizes a home, a home connotes a family, and we assume that family life began reasonably early in man's first two million years. Evidence concerning the nature of family life in primeval times is beyond recall, and the only recourse is to analogies, the inferences drawn both from what we know of tribal and modern peoples as well as from the studies of apes and monkeys. Many links obviously are missing, but it is an irresistible challenge to attempt a reconstruction of the beginning of family life among men. To date, the most thoughtful discussions of the problems involved have been offered by Phyllis C. Jay and S. L. Washburn.

The social ways of creatures on the threshold of manhood probably were dictated at first more by instincts than by learning. Along the line leading to man, however, there was a logarithmic expansion of learning experience which now has reached the point where instinct has entirely or almost entirely disappeared. The early observations of modern apes and monkeys in their natural habitats were made by untrained personnel who suggested that individual animals learn very little during their life spans. However, recent studies by well-trained observers demonstrate that considerable learning takes place during the life of an individual monkey or ape. For example, one large group of wild baboons in the Nairobi Park, Kenya, at one time could be approached easily by car; but then two of these baboons were shot from a car. The same group could not be approached by car even eight months later, in spite of the fact that they must have seen "harmless" cars frequently during the interim. The implication is that the animals had learned from a single unpleasant episode that a car was a potentially fatal hazard. It is unlikely that all of the baboons saw the murder, but those who had not were willing to accept the judgment of those who had. Modern studies of apes and monkeys repeatedly suggest that a wide range of behavioral flexibility is an inherited propensity in these animals. Such flexibility based on learning was no doubt critical in the emergence of man. Ranking high among the social qualities of these animals is a gregariousness which leads individuals to live in groups. The normal number of modern apes found together is likely to be small. Chimpanzees, sociable for apes, rarely number over nine individuals in a loosely organized group, and such aggregates have memberships which change frequently. Suggestively, sex was a significant social binder for our threshold humans, but its importance should not be overemphasized. Most females would spend their lives as infants, juveniles or as pregnant or nursing adults, conditions which would tend to limit their periods of sexual receptivity. Furthermore, judging from the sexual life of wild apes and monkeys, the adults do not normally copulate unless the female is in estrus. Possibly it was not until long after they began to assume other human behavioral qualities that these females became receptive throughout the year to copulatory contact. As this pattern emerged, social tensions decreased, and there was an accompanying increase in social stability which would be of adaptive value. Thus, something more than sex kept the first groups together, and this something was most likely the knowledge carried by the group.

The shared experience of the group would have adaptive value which could not be achieved by lone individuals. As learning increased, and as it became ever so cumulative, to be in the midst of others gained in value. Throughout his life each individual probably remained as a member of the band into which he had been born. The bands may have numbered from ten to fifty individuals as among most modern apes and monkeys. Within the band a number of interlocking dimensions reinforced social cohesion. As emerging ground-dwelling creatures who must survive among predators such as hyenas and lions, the adult males protected the females, infants, and juveniles. Those that wandered off alone, whether young or old, were sooner or later likely to become casualties. The fact that a single individual was no match for predators greatly strengthened group living. The sexual attractiveness of females served in part to keep males nearby, and the infants were linked to their mothers by an extended period of maturation. The social tie that would emerge eventually as most critical in the family life of humans was the mother-offspring association. The relatively long-term bonds between a modern ape mother and her offspring again are suggestive in terms of learning. In order to develop behavioral flexibility a long period of learning is required, with nourishment as well as protection provided by the mother. It is undoubtedly important that a female monkey or ape raised in isolation does not have the innate ability to care for an infant. The necessary skills are learned as the juvenile females play with infants and practice the mother role before attaining sexual maturity and motherhood. Furthermore, in the broader social group an infant comes to share the learning experiences of all the age categories to which it is exposed. For apes on the threshold of humanness we might assume that a close paired or dyadic relationship existed between a mother and her offspring for at least the first five postnatal years. During this period the mother could not move about as readily as a nonmother. Not only did females and their young decrease band mobility, but they required greater protection. Mothers and their young were a liability, and even though they formed the basic unit for perpetuating the band, they were tolerated only because of the species' social nature.

At this point in time we have every reason to think that breeding was within a band and was based on male dominance. Males competed with each other over females, but constant turmoil was avoided with the establishment of a pecking order. Once a male had fought and won or lost to another, the dominance pattern between the two was established. The loser might challenge his adversary at a later date but not until he felt rather certain that he could win and move up the ladder of strength. The young defeated males were forced to suppress their sexual desires, and natural selection favored the individuals who succeeded in doing so. The strongest males were the most frequent breeders, and because of their recognized strength the females, infants, and juveniles felt secure when physically near them. To demonstrate affection, and perhaps in order to obtain food, females freely submitted to the sexual advances of the powerful males and also groomed those males with whom they felt most secure. The females rubbed dirt from the skins of their "apes," picked lice from their hair, removed ticks and thorns from their bodies, and licked their wounds.

Crossing the divide from ape to man must have been a long and meandering process, but certain steps must have occurred even though we do not know in what order. One critical change took place when it became routine to establish a base camp from which adult males ranged during the day while all of the others remained at or near the camp. The females, their young, the juveniles, the injured, and the old searched nearby for plant foods and small animals, but most of the males wandered farther to gather plant products and, more importantly, to hunt game. When males began pursuing small game or young animals of larger species away from their base, they probably did not range far. This was the first step, however, in perfecting their stalking and killing abilities. The hunting of small animals is not very rewarding in terms of the meat harvest, and it would in time be realized that hunting large animals cooperatively could increase each person's take greatly. Cooperative hunting among males had another value, for it introduced a quality of mutual dependence which gave rise to an *esprit de corps* not only with respect to hunting but, by gradual extension, to all matters of mutual concern.

To take large game cooperatively must have required that the men range far from the females and others who remained at a base camp. After a group of hunters had been successful, they probably first butchered the freshly killed animals and ate the delicacies immediately. The next move would be either to send a messenger to the base camp to bring the women and children to the kill site or else the hunters would carry the meat to the base camp. If the animals taken were numerous and large, the base camp would be moved to the kill site. When either alternative was followed for the first time, beginning what would become a long-lasting pattern, we have another critical moment in man's development. The existence of conscious and reasoned concern with the welfare of those in the band who were not involved in the kill came into being. When this early sharing began, there already existed the social binders of gregariousness, sex, and group identity. The kill probably was divided among the hunters, with each man receiving a portion to feed those for whom he was responsible. In this manner the economic basis of a nuclear family may have come into being.

The band might stay at one camp for a single day or for a longer period if abundant food sources were nearby. In any case they ranged over a well-defined area rather than at random. By hunting and collecting in one sector they came to know where and when particular species were most likely to be available. If they were to wander about at random or forage in unknown localities, their chances of consistent success in subsistence activities would be reduced considerably. Therefore, they left a region only after locally available foods became insufficient; this might result from either a decrease in the environmental offering or an increase in the population size.

The ten to fifty individuals who lived together in a single camp were related closely in both genetic and social terms. Within this general relationship, the most lasting specific ties were the one between an infant and its mother and that between a dominant male and one or more females. The bond between mates was based on economic interests and sexual attractiveness, and it was the sexual ties and grooming which would lead to the more abstract human emotions of love and affection. In the development of human social consciousness the mother-child relationship must also have been a very early medium for the expression of warmth and affection.

The mating pattern of the early humans may be conceived broadly in terms of a number of particular and probable biological variables. We may assume that the menarche, or the first time a female menstruated, was near the age of twelve years. In all likelihood she would not be fertile for another year or two due to the factor of adolescent sterility. She would bear her first offspring by the time she was fifteen and would nurse it for about two years. The prolonged nursing period was necessary because the available food was too coarse to be digested by an infant or very small child. If the mother bore an offspring during the time she was nursing another child, the newborn might be killed. If the baby were not killed outright, the likelihood remained that it would die since a woman living in primitive conditions seldom could provide enough nourishment at one time for two nursing infants. Fifteen years after bearing her first child the mother probably was either dead or had reached her menopause and was out of the reproductive cycle. If the firstborn had been a male, he might mate with his mother toward the end of her reproductive span. However, this firstborn, as well as all other newborn infants, probably had only about a fifty-fifty chance of surviving the first year of life. If it did survive, if it were a boy, if the mother were alive and fertile, and if she was not pregnant, then her son might mate with her and she could conceive his progeny. If the firstborn had been a female, she might mate with a younger brother or with her father. In these terms it would appear that the mating and then the incest prohibitions within the basic or nuclear family, composed of a woman, her man and their children, arose for largely biological reasons. We might further suppose that it was the unlikelihood of being able to reproduce within the nuclear family except between the original mates that in time led to the social prohibition of marriages within the unit.

To suggest the reasons for the emergence of marriage as a social institution would be almost pure speculation, for again there is no evidence of its beginning stages. About all that can be said is that a relatively durable pairing of an adult male and a female is found in virtually all human societies and has proved to be an efficient means for perpetuating humans and culture. The complementary labors of a man and woman, the environment provided for teaching skills to the children, the emotional and sexual gratifications offered within the framework of marriage are each important in fostering its durability. We know too that choosing marriage partners from outside the band tended to provide secure and stable relations with adjacent peoples and probably represented the first successful "national treaties."

LANGUAGE Continuing the search for great moments in man's emergence we must recognize that the development of language was a giant step forward in the process of humanization. With respect to the origin of language, more links are apparent between the communication systems of land mammals in general and monkeys, apes, and man than can be recognized in the comparisons of family life or mating habits. All species in these groups share such critical characteristics as an ability to vocalize and reproduce particular sounds, or in other words, to speak and be heard within a particular range. Vocalization lingers only for a moment, does not usually interfere with other activities, and conveys arbitrary meanings. The unique quality of any language is that it includes only a small set of distinct sounds derived from the potential range of sounds. When a limited number of sounds are combined in a consistent manner, they come to convey arbitrary associations or meanings. Unlike the vocal signals of other animals, the words or combinations of words which men have learned to use make it possible for them to say, hear, and understand many clusters of sounds. They may even understand the meaning of a cluster of sounds which form a new combination, provided the sounds are grouped according to the specific patterns in that particular language. Furthermore, man alone has the ability to discuss events and objects that are displaced in time and space from the moment of vocalization.

Ape-men would have had a system of arbitrary signals that conveyed particular associations to the hearers from the speakers. Signals of this nature expressed the elemental feelings of danger, anger, affection, or pain. The hearers of the danger signal could not determine from its sounds, however, the specific nature of the threat, which might be fire, predators, or some other immediate hazard. A danger signal, like the others, was an auditory alerting method, but it required further visual clarification by the hearer. These creatures, at the threshold of humanness, not only possessed anatomical characteristics which permitted the vocalization of signals, but they also had the intellectual potential for further elaboration. At such a point in human time it is quite likely that some of the vocalized signals graded into one another, such as is currently the pattern reported from nonhuman primates, to convey general feelings or an observed condition; in this case the signals would be expressive rather than specifically referential. It is reasonable to suggest that the ability to communicate a danger signal had individual survival value. The prerequisites would be a neuropsychological system capable of creating a sound to convey the meaning of danger, the physical ability to produce this sound, and the intelligence to remember the meaning. The earliest vocalization would be in phonemic units composed of sounds intergraded with each other. The physiological potential for vocalizing distinct sounds and the mental ability to have a consistent combination of these express a particular meaning combined to create great biosocial advances. For example, we might imagine that a generalized danger signal became slightly modified into a variant form, and that this consistently indicated the presence of the most common predator. Even this simplest variation on a known sound, developed along with an ability to isolate it and remember its meaning, suggests the potential for infinite expansiveness. In this way anatomical abilities, memory, intelligence, and originality would combine to establish new sound patterns. The next step would be an ability to speak of something not present at the moment. To talk about a lion without seeing one, for example, made it possible for one person's learning experiences to be conveyed to another person through displaced memory. It is in this manner that the core of sociocultural experience began to accrue. The virtual magic of language developed when a unique combination of sounds became associated with any specific object or experience. Thus, only man can distinguish between wife and sister, between sin and sex, or Sunday and Funday.

In speculating about the origins and development of language, it should be considered quite possible that the men who manufactured Oldowan split pebble implements possessed culture but not language. At least, verbal skills would not be an essential ingredient in learning to make or use simple tools. To observe the manufacturing processes and attempt to duplicate them would be more important at this stage than to hear verbal descriptions of the steps involved. In the same context, learning to track and trap animals and then stone them to death probably was best accomplished by watching other hunters perform these activities. Through observation and practice, a novice could acquire the necessary skills for himself. Similarly, simple forms of band and family organization could have existed before the development of language. At the same time, it is difficult to imagine much complexity or flexibility in family or band life without language. By extension, the more abstract aspects of culture, oral literature and most of what is religion, require a well-developed language for understanding and transmission.

If culture and its carrier, man, arose at one time and in one place, as we might assume, then possibly all languages had a single origin. However, when men wandered away from a linguistic cradle in Africa, their language became diversified as one segment of the population became geographically separated from another. The result was the rise of only partially similar vocabularies and grammars, and these subsequently became distinct languages. As time passed verbal communication systems became increasingly capable of expressing complex personal thoughts. Each language acquired a vocabulary which expressed and reflected the interests of its speakers. Thus, some Eskimos have at least twenty different words to distinguish the variations in snow. In our society a similar proliferation of words exists and is used among cowboys for cows or among airplane pilots for weather conditions. Furthermore, the colloquial variations built around any symbolic concept will reflect even more the intensity of interests of the speakers. For example, given the American Breast Cult we note the accepted designations of breasts, bosom, or bust and the alternatives of boobies, boobs, cans, chest, front, grapefruit (as well as other fruits), handles, knobs, knockers, jugs, pods, teats, tits, and titty. In a similar vein we might consider the range of words for money or for policemen in our society. Although the alternative terms for breasts, money, and policemen are colloquial or slang expressions, they nonetheless are words in common usage, which makes them important in any realistic analysis of a language. An Eskimo who can make innumerable distinctions among the forms of snow could soon learn to express distinctions among cows or automobile styles if he lived where such distinctions were important. Thus the extensiveness of any aspect of a people's vocabulary depends on their cultural and social interests.

TECHNOLOGY The time has come for another look at manufactures, not only because their archeological remains are plentiful but also because much of our distinctive way of life today is technologically based. As mentioned earlier, anticipations of tool-making through the use of natural tools probably existed at the threshold of humanness. The first such usages are likely to have included stones employed as pounders or missiles, and sticks used as spears, clubs, probes, or diggers. In the earliest known stone technology, reported from Olduvai Gorge, Tanzania, not only were the prepared tools, such as the Oldowan split pebbles, utilized, but the flakes derived in the process also were used. A minimal production kit for stoneworking consisted of only the hammerstone necessary to detach flakes from a pebble; thus a single object was utilized to create a single tool type. Although there is no satisfactory association of culture with Java Man, such a connection may be made with the bones of Peking Man. In the caves near Choukoutien are not only the remains of fire and the bones of animals consumed but stone tools as well. These include flaked pebbles and pieces of quartzite which had been flaked to form choppers and scrapers. The stone tools are remarkably similar in form throughout the intermittent occupancy of the caves which spans as much as 300,000 years. Like the Oldowan tools, those from China probably were produced by using only hammerstones as flaking implements.

At Olduvai Gorge, superimposed on the Oldowan lithic complex, was a stoneworking tradition which extended from *Homo erectus* times into the era of modern man. The flaked stone artifacts comprise a lithic complex called Chellean-Acheulean, and the most characteristic tool produced was the hand ax, which did not go out of fashion until about 40,000 years ago. The hand ax was made from an oblong pebble; in its most basic form, flakes were removed from both sides at one end to produce a blunted point. As in the case of Oldowan split pebbles, the hand axes appear to have been fashioned with hammer-stones as the only production tool. In the early stages of the hand-ax tradition, during Chellean times (alternatively termed Abbevillian), much of the smooth, original surface of a pebble was not modified; large flakes were removed only from one end. At the lowest Chellean levels hand axes were scarce, and the Oldowan pebbles were the most numerous worked-stone forms. Later in the strata hand axes dominated, and they became increasingly well made as time passed. The latter part of the Chellean lithic tradition merges into the Acheulean, and at this time hand axes with further technical refinements were produced. The large flakes continued to be removed with heavy blows from a hammerstone, but the cutting surfaces were finished by striking more controlled and lighter blows with a roundheaded flaking tool which probably was made from bone or horn. The discovery of this refining method led to the production of small, thin hand axes with an accompanying economy in the amount of material used. Throughout its span the hand ax was a multipurpose implement. It probably was held in the hand, and it could be used as a weapon or as an implement to dig in the ground, cut meat, smash bones, and possibly to rough out wooden artifacts. The hand ax was a simple but highly versatile tool, and it served man for a longer span of time than any of his other manufactures.

As the Acheulean waned, another lithic production skill was developed. This involved the manufacture of one stone form from which a second, the desired end product, was derived. The Acheulean flint knappers developed the ability to chip away at a small piece of flint until they had fashioned it into a particular type of core (Levallois core). They then detached a flake from one particular portion of the core to produce a blade for a backed knife (Figure 8). The remarkable nature of the Levalloisian flake knife, or tortoise-backed blade, is that the flint worker conceptualized an end product which necessitated three steps before completion, another important first in the development of stone technology. The tortoise-backed blade was a highly efficient knife, and the technique of its production was perfected fully by Mousterian times, which ranged from 80,000 to 40,000 years ago.

Mousterian sites in France yield some thirty-five different forms of stone tools which archeologists interpret as having served distinct purposes. By this time man was so skilled in flaking stone by the percussion technique that he could experiment in making new forms; of even more importance, he exhibited pride of workmanship by

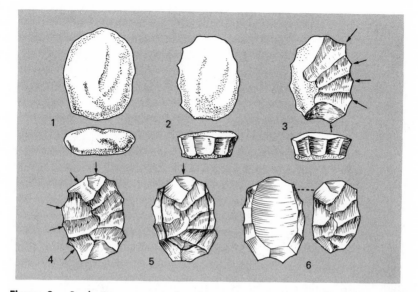

Figure 8. *Production sequence for the production of a Levallois flake knife (Courtesy of Francois Bordes, "Mousterian Cultures in France," Science, v. 134, no. 3482, 1961).*

producing tools chipped to a degree of perfection far beyond that which was required for the purposes they served. Mousterian percussion-flaked tools represent a culmination in one stoneworking tradition. No radical change in stone technology would take place until man learned the technique of applying pressure to remove very small flakes from the item being manufactured. Only then would more diverse and finer stone tools be produced. It might be emphasized here that each material and the methodology for working it have built-in or natural limitations. Flint and other stones with similar qualities may be processed only in a limited number of ways, and so it is with every other material in the natural world. This statement may not seem striking, but its implications are. It means that in every substance, such as stone, wood, plastics, and metals, there are inherent qualities limiting its service to man. In this respect the gross dimensions of technological achievement are limited by the materials available.

Another technological achievement of Mousterian times had even greater short- and long-range implications in manufacturing. From his beginnings man is presumed to have used sharp-pointed sticks as spears and rocks as missiles. Well before Mousterian times, small pieces of flint flaked into the form of elongated triangles served as knives. Men of Mousterian times possibly were the first persons, however, to attach a piece of flaked stone to the end of a stick and thereby produce a spear with a sharp cutting point. The implications of this addition to human knowledge are earthshaking. The innovation must have altered man's hunting methods drastically, since a stone-tipped spear could be thrown or could be held in the hand to keep an animal at bay until it could be stabbed fatally. Likewise the stone-tipped spear brought about a revolution in the settling of conflicts between men; combat which literally had been hand-to-hand now could be replaced by more decisive spear-to-spear confrontations. (We might even conjecture that such a weapon was considered so devastating and deadly that a moratorium was declared against its use between men as the first international agreement. An ultimate weapon such as this clearly would destroy all of mankind, and Mousterian men were men with intelligence. We might imagine too that some barbarians improved on the stone-tipped spear ever so slightly and could not resist using their superior weapon against their fellowmen. In this manner the ultimate weapon became an accepted means for settling human conflicts, as old people shook their heads and doubted that their grandchildren could possibly survive in such a mad world.) Neanderthal man, who in his classic physical form occupied much of Europe for a comparatively brief span of time, is most often associated with these Mousterian tools which, in terms of one stoneworking tradition, represent an apex in a long series of cumulative achievements.

This brief history of tool-making by advances in stone chipping has been introduced in order to examine the implications of man's first great venture into technology. Although the details of the transition from one artifact type to the next are obscure and only the most critical forms are mentioned here, a number of points are abundantly clear. The first is that of all the materials available to the first men, one was selected because of its inherently suitable properties. Presumably the first men unknowingly searched for a durable substance, one which could serve as an extension of human teeth. Experiments were made with bone, but its brittleness and failure to retain a sharp edge made it ineffective as a cutting-tool material. It was discovered that some stones cut well when chipped, particularly those such as flint which produce a concoidal fracture. Materials of this nature were increasingly sought since men could utilize only those living and dead materials which surrounded them. Thus it is that man's tools depended on materials from the natural world. Technology would have developed differently if nature had produced a raw material which had the plastic qualities of clay when moist but hardened naturally to the sharpness of flint. Only by attempting to conceive of a substance such as this may we begin to realize the limitations inherent in the materials available to man from nature.

The vastness of the time span when the Oldowan split pebbles remained unchanged in form and were the most important stone tools suggests that once a successful model was conceived it was likely to persist for a long time. In that era at the dawn of human time, men in all likelihood did not possess the reasoning abilities of men today, which helps to explain the persistence of split pebbles as tools. The hand ax too existed for a long time, but the span of its popularity was brief in comparison with that of Oldowan split pebbles, from which the hand ax probably was derived. We see a cumulative increase in the complexity of stonework from split pebbles to early and then later hand ax forms, followed by the later development of the backed knife-blade. We may quite legitimately refer to this developmental sequence as the evolution of technological achievements in stoneworking, since each stage emerged from the previous one. If there is evolution in stoneworking abilities, apparent because of the changes in the finished products, we may expect that other manifestations of human activity also have an evolutionary development. In these terms there would be evolution in sociocultural behaviors just as there is biological evolution in all living organisms.

The Mousterian stone technology not only represents an apex in a long series of cumulative achievements but indicates another direction in which technology will move. Here is the first clear-cut example of a material with one set of physical properties, stone, being joined by man to something else with very different qualities, wood. By combining the flexible, wood, with the solid, stone, a composite artifact, the stone-tipped spear, became a reality. The scientific and technical potential of this conjunction of different materials had vast and lasting implications in the development of artifacts. There is a great potential of variety and complexity in the many possible combinations of materials. Metal bonded to plastic, wood joined with paper, metal attached to paper, or paint applied to ceramics exemplify the potentialities in the combinations of materials with disparate inherent properties. Quite obviously, much of our technological sophistication is derived from the type of conjunction seen first in Mousterian stone-wood spears.

Other technological trends evident by Mousterian times include the more careful selection of raw materials and, more importantly, the decrease in size of the well-established artifact forms. The hand axes were not only better made and more varied than ever before, but they also were much smaller. These attributes suggest that the medium of workmanship had become considerably refined. In addition, the size of some forms tended to be reduced as knowledge about the material or materials of which they were composed increased. The miniaturization of much of the equipment contained in missiles is a contemporary example of this lasting trend.

The evolution of stoneworking, seen in the refinement of percussion flaking to produce more complex, diverse, and diminutive forms, was continued as the technique of stone chipping itself changed. This great innovation centered on applying pressure with a horn tool to achieve greater precision in removing chips from an artifact after its gross form had been blanked out with the percussion technique. By the Chatelperronian era centering some 30,000 years ago, pressure flaking had become more important than the percussion technique, but it did not reach its greatest elaboration until about 8000 B.C. By this time the potential variability in flaked stone tools had been virtually exhausted. Thus, some 10,000 years ago most of the possible variations in chipped stone tool technology had been realized. Some peoples around the world continue today to flake stone in styles that are over 20,000 years old, whereas other peoples long ago began to explore the potentialities of new and vastly different mediums. The workmanship in copper, iron, and steel would follow much the same historical line of development that prevailed for stone. Despite the inherently different qualities of the new materials employed, the cumulative pattern is from the simple to complex, from gross to refined, from sameness to diversity. It is in directions such as these that technology and suggestively all aspects of cultural behavior have been moving for the last two million years.

5

HUMAN NATURE
AND CONFLICT

As we conceive of human nature, it is a product of our thinking rather than a collection of autonomous activities. Very little behavior in humans is inborn, because what is innate in other animals has been replaced in man almost entirely by learned responses. The human behaviors most often cited as instinctive are a fear of loud noises and an ability to suck, but these characteristics may in fact be learned prenatally. Even human behavior which is physiologically based includes little of a truly spontaneous nature. For example, all men belch because of their biological processes. The gas rises because of a physiological process, but the way in which it is accommodated at its oral exit may be conditioned culturally. An Eskimo belches often and with gusto but does not give the matter even a passing thought. We, on the other hand, do our best to avoid belching noticeably; to us, even the word is mildly offensive. If our controls cannot restrain the gas, it emerges as a discrete "burp," which those hearing it attempt to ignore. One culture may dictate the way to render a belch, to yawn, or to scratch an itch, while another may not regard these as matters of concern. Even whispered inquiries about the normal manner in which to handle almost any overt aspect of a physiological process soon reveal that people somewhere have an attitude toward the process which differs from our own. Thus arises the suggestion that responses of this nature are learned, even in those facets of human behavior which we often think of as autonomous. This point becomes important in considering whether certain behaviors are alterable by cultural means or whether changes must be at a genetic level.

DRIVES Men are fundamentally animals, biological beings who must in some way perform a cluster of particular activities because of their organic nature. We have *primary drives* or impulses on which our physiological well-being depends. An *ingestion drive* for air, food, and water is clearly a very basic requirement, and yet its fulfillment is molded by culture. The clean desert air which the Navajo Indians of Arizona breathed was quite different from the stale, fetid atmosphere to which an Alaskan Eskimo man was accustomed in his men's house. Nonetheless, each group accepts the quality of its air as part of the normal environment. In a like manner, food thought by one people to be a necessity remains unacceptable to others; even the amount of water thought to be vital varies widely between peoples in desert and temperate settings. Along with ingestion, an *excretion drive* exists to rid the body of such waste substances as urine, feces, and other residues. As a cultural concern, excreting is less dominant than ingesting, but it may become a subject for considerable attention. The people in some societies have rigid rules about the appropriate times and places to urinate or defecate, whereas these matters are of only passing concern to another people. The odors of perspiration or of exhaled air are ignored by most peoples, and yet others focus attention on these matters. The final primary drive is toward the *avoidance* of heat, cold, and pain. The tolerance limit for each is set by our biological nature, but once again culture molds the reaction level of any society's members. Cold evokes a reaction from a Caucasian living in a temperate region different from that of an Eskimo, because the Eskimo, although he has much the same biological response, has a very different cultural attitude toward cold. Such differences likewise are found in reactions to heat and pain. Thus, in man the processes of ingestion, excretion, and avoidance have physiological limitations, but they also are regulated by standards of accommodation which are culturally determined.

It is not difficult to imagine that hunting game animals and collecting plant foods are responses to the primary drive of ingestion; that men built shelters and houses to avoid heat and cold; or that public toilets serve the excretion drive. However, there is a vast area of human interests which has no direct nor very clear connection with primary drives. This behavioral spectrum may be termed *secondary drives*, which are above all else the product of a particular culture and

tion, withdrawal, or violence—the prisoner reflects cultural and personal conditioning to particular stresses, and violence in such a situation would be no more instinctive than would be the alternatives of cooperation and withdrawal.

AGGRESSION AND TRIBAL PEOPLES Stress is a normal part of living, and nothing is unnatural about responding to it. During aggressive play or "pseudo-violence" such as rough-housing, a child learns the acceptable limits of personal contact and pain infliction just as he later learns the dominance and submission pattern of his culture with respect to other aspects of social interaction. A child soon learns his culture's code for acceptable aggression. A four-year-old Eskimo boy is taught that he should not strike another boy, and by the time he is eight he does not do so. However, he finds that he may beat a chained dog with a heavy stick, even if the dog has done nothing wrong. Although he does not realize it, the boy is learning that he must cooperate with other males in his village, especially age-mates with whom he will interact throughout his life, and that his aggression is to be directed instead against animals. As he matures, his animal-directed aggression serves as a primary means for furthering survival.

When men subsisted by hunting and killing animals for food, many of their stresses could be released by violent actions against animals. Gastric and emotional tensions were fulfilled and released when an animal was murdered and later consumed. Hunger stress conceivably could lead to the murder and consumption of infants, plump young children, or others within the group if animal killing were inadequate, but if this occurred, band cohesion and cooperation in normal social life or hunting would be jeopardized.

It is reasonable to suppose that the earliest men could not have perpetuated themselves if they habitually, or even occasionally, ate members of their own band. Infant deaths from natural causes probably were high under the best of circumstances, and although infants would have provided the tenderest meat, they also were the only hope for the future. Members of one band would not ordinarily hunt and kill individuals in adjoining bands, for such peoples were bound by ties of blood and marriage through the exchange of spouses. Serious or constant conflicts with adjacent peoples would have led to a future almost as uncertain as that which would result from killing one's own children. Close cooperation within a band and intermittent cooperation with adjacent bands was accompanied, however, by conflicts with more distant bands, whose members, since they were culturally different, might be considered as game to be killed and consumed. Once again, it probably was not instinct but a frustration of the aggressor's primary drives which led to violence against these distant peoples, and the forms of such violence had evolved from learned hunting behavior.

The earliest men, as hunters and foragers, were most likely to survive by frequenting a limited geographical area which contained diverse resources. The yearly cycle in nature made it possible for them to know the optimum times and places to search for the particular foods prevalent in the region. Even prehuman bands had learned to limit their foraging to a well-defined territory. The advantages of wandering over a limited area versus wandering freely are obvious. Gatherers ranging repeatedly over the same ground would come to know the habitats of local plants or animals, and this familiarity would have greater survival value than would expansion into new and unfamiliar lands. Only when food resources became inadequate in an area of traditional exploitation did wandering people venture elsewhere. Thus, the pattern of territoriality arose not from instinct but from the recognized economic advantage of restricting one's area of habitual exploitation. It often is asked whether territoriality, since it is found among most animals, is not a basic characteristic of living organisms. It is basic only insofar as it is the most efficient method of survival in most environments and therefore prevails among many diverse species.

If war is defined as organized armed conflict between societies, it clearly was known to most tribal peoples in the world. In a technical sense, war did not exist among a few peoples around the world. For example, the Polar Eskimos who lived in northwestern Greenland did not know of war when they were discovered in 1818. These Eskimos had lost all contact with other peoples and thought that they were the only humans in the world. Nonetheless, the Polar Eskimos did fight among themselves, usually over women, and these animosities led to rather frequent feuds and murders. The reasons cited in the literature for warfare among primitives are so diverse that we may query any single instinct as being the compelling cause for groups of men to harm one another.

Among early tribal peoples the factor frequently leading to violence may have been the drive to ingest. The availability of air and water was seldom critical, but a scarcity of food might cause stress and frustrations which would lead to war. Insufficient food produced actual physical stress which, if severe enough, led to social tensions within a tribe. These conditions sometimes forced people to range beyond the periphery of the area which they exploited habitually, and this imposition on another tribe's territory often led to warfare. Only those groups who had arrived at ways to limit their population artificially or who had their numbers restricted by factors beyond their control found such encroachment unnecessary. As an example, assume that a small tribe of hunters lived in an area with a limited supply of meat animals. The hunters would learn to exploit efficiently their prime source of food, and sooner or later they might reach a point at which population growth outstripped the productivity of the area. If no other peoples lived nearby, they would expand peaceably into unoccupied areas and in time duplicate the situation which had prevailed in the home territory of their ancestors. With a further passage of time all lands would become occupied, and if population outstripped food supply then, the situation would require new and different solutions. The population might be controlled by practicing abortion or infanticide. Other means to accomplish the same end might include a restriction against the marriage of adult males until they are advanced in age, or an encouragement for individuals to remain unmarried throughout their lives. A society of hunters which had these or other similar population controls in operation before a period of critical food shortage might intensify their application rather than consider expanding beyond their traditional area of exploitation. It must be mentioned that low population numbers were characteristic of many societies. This resulted from natural causes such as high infant mortality, famines, or periodic epidemics, and made territorial expansion unnecessary. It often is stated that Eskimos were among the least warlike of aboriginal peoples. Among them infant mortality was high, infanticide sometimes was practiced, accidental deaths were common, and famines were not unusual. Because they had a difficult time even sustaining their own number at home, they exerted little or no pressure on the lands of others.

If in times of food stress a small-scale society could not artificially adjust its number, its members might attempt to overcome nearby peoples and occupy their land. Since tribal societies usually were ethnocentric and regarded strangers as essentially nonhuman, it was not difficult for them to justify such violence. The wars which ensued always were "won," insofar as they resolved the problem of imbalance between population and resources. If they defeated an enemy, the aggressors could then exploit their conquered lands. If the aggressors were defeated, their number would have been reduced by the conflict, and this would eliminate the food stress. Thus, even in defeat, warfare alleviated this type of physical tension.

Although frustration of the primary drive for food was no doubt responsible for much of the aggression among early tribal peoples, other stress situations arose within bands and resulted in either withdrawal, cooperation, or aggression. Presentation of the frustration responses of the Andaman Islanders, an example of a small-scale society which existed into modern times, will illustrate the alternatives of action developed among one people. Around 1860 the Andaman Islands, in the Bengal Sea between the Malay Peninsula and India, were inhabited by some 5000 Negritos, known in the literature as the Andamanese. They are a black-skinned, frizzy-haired population of very short stature. These Negritos subsisted mainly on sea turtles if they lived along the coasts or on turtles and wild pigs if they ranged from the coasts into the dense jungles. Effective European contacts were made with many of the Andamanese in the nineteenth century, but some of the people still retained their traditional ways when studied by the anthropologist A. R. Radcliffe-Brown from 1906 to 1908. Without offering details about their way of life let us note that their inventory of material manufactures was very limited, they ranged in small groups over localized areas, and they camped at first one spot and then another, returning intermittently to a base camp. The Andamanese are among the least complex hunters who have survived into modern times.

Andamanese political organization was minimal, and the traditional concepts of power and authority are not appropriate for describing their pattern of relationships between men. Rather than formal chiefs, they had leaders accepted informally. These men of wisdom and experience exercised a nonauthoritative influence over fellow band members. A leader could not coerce, punish, or command; he recommended or advised and was heeded because of his knowledge. Conflicts appear to have resulted most often from personal injury, theft, adultery, or property damage. When two men of the same camp quarrelled, as sometimes happened, profanity was exchanged, and one man might even shoot an arrow near the other or destroy any property at hand, including his own. In a situation such as this the women, children, and even some men fled fearfully into the jungle. A leader who spoke up, however, usually was able to calm the emotions of those involved, and as a result direct violence against another person was avoided. In rare instances, however, a murder would occur. The killer then left the site and hid in the jungle, where he was joined by those who sympathized with him. Revenge depended on the friends and relatives of the dead man, but if the murderer succeeded in avoiding them for a few months, he could rejoin the group because people forgot or forgave such murders after a short span of time. More serious was the murder of someone from another local band because this led to feuds. Conflicts of this nature were perpetuated, but not settled, by surprise attacks, the murder of one or two persons, and a quick retreat. If the victims retaliated effectively or if the attackers lost one of their party, the raid ended in withdrawal. Feuds were settled eventually through women who served as the intermediaries between the contesting groups.

Ethnographic accounts of the Andaman Islanders suggest that violence was uncommon and that its most extreme form, murder, was rare. Clearly, withdrawal was a fully acceptable course of action in dealing with aggressive behavior. Mutual adjustments and cooperation also were common means for settling differences, but sometimes these solutions could be applied only following violence or temporary withdrawal. The violence which did occur among the Andamanese arose from shared social stresses or at times because of individual pathology. It was set in motion by secondary drives of social and cultural origins rather than by primary needs. The sociocultural system could not accommodate the frustrations of everyone with tranquillity, and in these terms it was not perfect. However, because of individual tolerance and because withdrawal or cooperation were the more culturally acceptable reactions, violence remained of minor importance as a means of dealing with frustrations.

Other societies might be cited in which in-group violence was even less frequent than among the Andamanese. The Hopi Indians of northeastern Arizona are an example. These pueblo-dwelling farmers avoided shedding blood, and even their methods for killing animals were as bloodless as possible. For a Hopi to kill a member of his own settlement was almost unknown. They were even reluctant to kill known enemies from near or far because of the supernatural dangers involved. All was not tranquil among the Hopi, however, despite their disapproval of physical violence. They gossiped viciously; their backbiting was almost institutionalized. Furthermore, individuals were constantly afraid of death by supernatural means because they believed that Hopi witches killed others in order to prolong their own lives, and one was never quite certain who was a witch. Even closely related adults or the children of a witch were not safe from such action. Thus, although there was little of the in-group or external physical violence found in most societies, there was at the same time considerable frustration, trauma, and hostility because of their supernatural system of beliefs.

In order to avoid skewing the discussion of violence in small-scale societies, it is desirable to cite a tribal people who are at present extraordinarily bellicose. The first contacts with a sterling example, the Yanomamo (Ya̧nomamö), were made in 1950, but most of the interactions between them and Euro-Americans postdate 1958. The Yanomamo live in Venezuela and Brazil along the upper Orinoco River, and between 1964 and 1968 the anthropologist Napoleon A. Chagnon spent nineteen months among them. The population of 10,000 is spread over a vast jungle area, with none of the small settlements including more than 250 persons. Most food comes from their gardens, but they also hunt monkeys, wild pigs, tapir, and other species.

The Yanomamo men are almost unbelievably violent, and the high value placed on physical aggression is instilled in males during early childhood. By the age of four a little boy already has learned that he may give full vent to his temper and may strike anyone in anger. He is teased and provoked until he hits someone, even his father, and then he is cheered and praised for his fierce nature. As an adult a man expects his wife to anticipate his needs in such ways as preparing a meal soon after he has returned from hunting. As mild punishment for failure in this respect, the husband may strike her with his hand or a piece of firewood. It is much more serious if a wife is known to be adulterous or is suspected of such behavior. She may be shot with a barbed arrow in the legs or buttocks, burned with a firebrand, or cut with a knife; in rare instances, she may be killed. One of their customs is for the men of one settlement to invite the people of nearby villages to feasts. After eating, the men hold individual pounding duels, during which one man strikes another on the chest as powerfully as possible with his clenched fist. Tempers rise as the blows increase, and the participants may string their bows with war arrows and prepare for an anticipated battle. If the hostility between two settlements has been great, the acceptance of an invitation to a feast might result in an ambush and massacre. Other aspects of their lives are equally as fraught with violence since this is their primary means of responding to stresses.

The Yanomamo justify their violence in terms of a myth about a moon man. He visited the earth to eat the souls of children, but two earthly brothers became offended at this behavior and shot at him with arrows. One brother's barbed arrow caused the moon man to bleed, and as his blood dropped to earth it became men, the Yanomamo. Their devotion to war is said to be a result of this creation from blood and violence. In anthropological terms, the causes of their warfare are more directly the result of their social behaviors. These people practice female infanticide frequently since they desire sons. As a result, there may be as many as thirty percent more males than females in a settlement. Potential wives are scarce not only because of female infanticide but also because powerful men have multiple wives. To make this situation even more complex, a man can select his wife only from among his female cross-cousins (mother's brothers' or father's sisters' daughters). Therefore, some men must remain bachelors well into their adult life, and their sexual gratification must come from married women since girls marry shortly after puberty. The taboo on sexual intercourse with pregnant or nursing women makes a married man's sex life much the same as that of bachelors although men do not rigidly adhere to the noncoitus taboo during the three-year nursing period. Given these conditions, adultery is not at all unusual, and it leads to vicious fights within a settlement. Larger villages offer more opportunities for sexual adventures but consequently are characterized by more fights. The village may split into smaller units, but then the members of each fragment are easier prey for nearby enemies who are in a position to demand women and back up their demands with force.

It certainly appears that the Yanomamo, like some contemporary tribal peoples in the highlands of New Guinea, are on a "cultural jag" of violence. The Yanomamo pattern of aggression is among men, and the number of individuals killed is not great although the threat of violent death is ever present. While ferocity is the norm, it must at the same time be realized that violence is controlled and channelled so that it climaxes in murders less often than in physically painful but nonlethal duels. Apparently their sociocultural system is highly successful and shows no signs of internal collapse; thus in this instance we have a rather clear example of a lasting way of life in which internal conflict has become stabilized.

Although physical conflicts between tribal peoples were known throughout most of the primitive world, the frequency and intensity of such tribal wars usually were balanced by the intertribal cooperation carried on regularly through trade relations. Given the differential resources over even a restricted geographical area, it is not surprising that raw materials were traded widely from one tribe to the next. Trading usually was on a person-to-person basis, which required planned meetings and at least a certain degree of trust in the persons with whom one traded. Food products probably were exchanged less often than raw materials or finished artifacts, but all three types of commodity bound peoples to each other. Trade relations accomplished a number of related purposes. Barter for a raw material such as very fine flint made it possible to have better weapons, and this led to the likelihood of greater success in the food quest. A trade in such luxury items as amber or shells satisfied secondary cultural drives. Equally as important was the fact that through trade foreigners came to be known. This expanded the area of safe contacts and also brought the realization that the people in different tribes were often really very much alike.

ULTIMATE VIOLENCE AND OURSELVES It was suggested earlier that Mousterian men developed an ultimate weapon, the stone-pointed spear, which some group among them could not resist using against other men. I would assume that the same conditions prevailed when the bow and arrow became an effective weapon about 20,000 years ago. By the time firearms were developed, weapons were man-killers first and foremost since by then most of the world's peoples were farmers and industrialists who did not depend on wild animals for food. All of the effective weapons developed by man have been used at some time to kill other men, and ultimate weapons are those which at any time period have the greatest practical kill potential. Their use has always been justified, correctly or not, by the "need" to defeat a merciless enemy. In this context I must expand on the need the United States felt to drop the first atomic bomb on such an enemy.

On August 6, 1945, an atomic bomb was dropped on the city of Hiroshima, Japan. At that time the population of this city was approximately 250,000, and of this number nearly 80,000 persons were killed as the bomb burst in air without the benefit of a rocket's red glare. Contrary to possible expectations, I will not moralize about the aftermath of this event, nor do I propose to describe the horror of the scene. Instead, I intend to discuss the prelude to the event, to recapitulate what transpired prior to that moment in history. Social scientists in the United States had studied the war situation and offered rational evaluations and recommendations, but they were unable to make their knowledge effective. The fact that they tried but failed is something which should be remembered unto the end of our time, and this critical failure should be well understood in its human and institutional dimensions.

Early in 1944 the Foreign Morale Analysis Division was organized within the Office of War Information to provide services to the departments of Navy, State, and War. The staff of thirty individuals included anthropologists, psychiatrists, and sociologists. The head of the Foreign Morale Analysis Division was Alexander H. Leighton, a psychiatrist and anthropologist. The assigned task of division personnel was to assess the psychological and sociological capacities of the Japanese to conduct the war effectively. A background perspective was gained by studying ethnographic materials about the Japanese, by reviewing their history, motion pictures, novels, and travel accounts, and by interviewing Japanese in the United States. In order to evaluate conditions current in 1944, the Division members studied captured diaries, letters, and official documents; evaluated reports by neutrals living in Japan; assessed prisoner-of-war interrogation reports, and gained added insight by studying the texts of Japanese newspapers, periodicals, and radio broadcasts. Their findings were dichotomized into those which applied to military personnel and those which pertained to the civilian population.

Among the key factors to be determined about Japanese military personnel was whether their soldiers would surrender in significant numbers and whether they could be induced to reveal useful information. The stereotypic view prevailing among Americans at the time was that the Japanese had developed an ideal type of soldier, one judged to be fearless, devoted to the point of fanaticism, and suicidal because of training and religion. This view of the Japanese military personnel probably was purposefully stressed in order to sustain a fighting spirit among American soldiers, induce civilians to contribute everything possible to the war effort, and counteract the prewar feeling that the Japanese were a polite, hard-working, and harmless people. From their earliest studies the Division personnel concluded that the morale of Japanese soldiers generally was high but was not consistently so. Factors which contributed to this high morale were faith in the Emperor and his divine power, faith in the home-front's effort to sustain them; faith in the righteousness of their cause, and faith in victory. By the spring of 1944 the long-term physical privations, inadequate weapons and decreasingly effective field support, and lack of confidence in the information they received all contributed to a deterioration in the morale of the soldiers. These cracks in the Japanese military effort were revealed clearly by the Division studies. At this time, some U.S. military leaders favored an expansion of the propaganda program to promote the surrender of Japanese soldiers, whereas others opposed it. The propaganda efforts included distributing leaflets and broadcasting news and cultural programs to the Japanese troops in the field in order to decrease their faith if not induce them to surrender. The Division study concluded that the program could be made much more effective if allied troops could be persuaded to take the Japanese soldiers who attempted to surrender as prisoners rather than to kill them. It appears that allied soldiers retained the view that the Japanese soldiers were suicidal fanatics, and therefore they did not attempt to induce individuals to surrender. The Japanese soldiers saw their companions shot by the allies when they offered themselves as prisoners, and this increased Japanese resistance and actually led them to suicidal behavior when they might not have acted so otherwise. Thus, the propaganda campaign appears to have failed at least in part because allied troops in the field could not be induced to comply with their role in it. This left the false impression that the enemy's soldiers were indeed difficult to defeat by conventional methods of warfare.

The assessment which prevailed among the allies concerning home-front morale was that the Japanese nation was solidly behind the war effort and that civilians were performing well. According to a Division report late in 1944, however, homefront morale had been high but was deteriorating. By early January of 1945 the Division judged this condition to be much worse in terms of war effort efficiency, and they expected "a blowup of some kind." This conclusion was reached after noting several factors: shifts were occurring in key personnel; students, factory workers, and Christians were used as scapegoats to help explain failures; the news from the fighting front was bad, and evacuations from cities were producing additional privations. The report concluded that a significant number of Japanese felt that they had lost the war, people were apathetic toward the war effort, and there was widespread fear of what would happen when the allies invaded Japan. This report angered some Office of War Information officials, who thought it inaccurate, but by March it had become apparent that the allied military planners were the ones who had an incorrect view of life in Japan. In the spring of 1945 Division personnel discussed these and related points with the policy makers. A report prepared in May once again set forth the Division's conclusions. However, the Office of War Information's Deputy Director for the Far East, Japanese Section, held up release of the report until the Division had agreed to modify its conclusions. On June 1, 1945, the revised report was released. When the conclusions of this report were compared with information obtained at the end of the war, they were proven remarkably accurate on major points. For example, it was learned then that by December 1944 the Japanese were losing all hope of winning the war and that a decision to surrender was made in May 1945. The Division report of June had anticipated that the Japanese would make real overtures toward peace and that if the war effort of the allies continued with no changes, the Japanese would surrender between July and September of 1945. The postwar survey indicated that they had planned to surrender before November 1, 1945—even if no atomic bombs had been dropped, even if the Russians had not entered the war, and even if no invasion of Japan had been planned. The inevitable conclusion from the Division's report of June 1945 and from the U.S. Strategic Bombing Survey made after the war, is that Japan would have surrendered by November without the United States having used its ultimate weapon, the atomic bomb.

All wars bring forth a host of honest but conflicting judgments about enemies. It seems apparent that in this instance, however, the opinion that there was a "need" to defeat a merciless enemy by using an ultimate weapon was unjustified. The point to be remembered is that Division attempts to present a factual resumé were thwarted because their carefully drawn *conclusions* would make the *opinions* prevalent among the military planners seem unjustified and unsound.

ALTERNATIVES TO VIOLENCE AMONG OURSELVES   Although it may be impossible to prove satisfactorily that violence is not an innate type of response to stress among humans, it is nonetheless clear that alternative reactions are possible and that there is no species-wide uniformity of context for violence. All men may at some time become violent, but the patterning of their violence is cultural rather than genetic. To attribute a "killer-instinct" to man is to range beyond the limits of present-day knowledge, but the idea has a great deal of appeal to some persons because it offers them an escape from responsibility and reason. Some persons, perhaps many, would like to think that when men act violently, they are being consumed by forces over which they have no conscious control. If seriously accepted, this rationale could lead to the destruction of all mankind. It is, however, far more reasonable to view most acts of muderous violence as unnatural or distorted human behavior. An awareness of behavioral abnormalities, whether individual or group, makes it possible in our modern world to treat the earlier stages of disequilibrium before violent acts are committed. Withdrawal symptoms or indications of aggressive build-ups are known to signal subsequent eruptions of violence if the frustrations are not resolved by cooperative means.

If violence is not an inborn quality in man, as I suspect it is not, it should be reckoned with as learned and patterned cultural behavior wherever it occurs—except when it is a manifestation of individual pathology such as brain damage, tumors, other diseases affecting reasoning abilities, or abnormal inheritance. By and large, if normal men can learn violence and murder, they have an equal potential for unlearning it and replacing it with culturally approved substitutes. Tribal hunting peoples most often directed their violent tendencies toward animals and their milder aggressive feelings into games, gossip, arguments, ridicule, mock-warfare, or similar actions. Conflicts with other peoples arose in part as competition for land and its resources increased; it was often empty stomachs which sent men abroad to fight other men. After most men became farmers and could produce reliable surpluses of food, human stresses causing aggression changed from those derived from primary drives to others built around secondary drives. Wars then were fought not so much for food but for cultural ambition and honor.

We find that acceptable outlets for aggression are more complex in our society because of the nature of our cultural elaborations. Gossip, ridicule, and mockery are expanded in their dimensions and utilized to an elaborate degree. The scandalmongering of some syndicated newspaper columnists; the antagonisms exposed in some television interviews; the prickly exchanges on "conversation" radio programs, and the statements by politicians about each other offer written, verbal, and visual examples of vicarious substitutes for personalized aggression. We lack the mock-warfare of tribal peoples, but many of our television programs offer visual portrayals of violence. Other dimensions to vicarious violence include motion pictures based on monster, cowboy, and other violent themes. On the printed pages of books we find that Mike Hammer and James Bond are towering representatives of the violence school in fiction. The sale of books about these two individuals is astronomical, a clear indication of their appeal to millions. Perhaps the drawings of Goya owe at least part of their lasting appeal to the brutal violence he portrayed so realistically. It even seems that much of the durability of Euro-American fairytales is based on their themes of violence.

Some competitive national sports clearly appeal largely because of their approved and structured quasi-violence. Football and prizefighting come to mind first, but wrestling, roller derby, ice hockey, and auto racing must not be ignored. The Olympic Games represent this sporting competition internationally, with the emphasis on the number of victories achieved by competing nations. In the category of approved violence must be included the "sportsmen" who as hunters slaughter untold numbers of birds and mammals. The drawback to these outlets, apart from hunting, as a vent for aggressive feelings is that such fulfillment can be vicarious only, or in the case of athletic sports vicarious for all except the few players. The release of stress vicariously does not appear to be adequate in many cases and may, in fact, stimulate violent actions on the part of some observers.

We as individuals in the United States are well-known in the Western world for at least tacitly approving personal violence between individuals. Life on the frontier with a man's gun as the "law," the lynch mobs in the South not so very long ago, and the current murders each day are clear evidence for the on-going and very viable nature of our propensity for violence. Admitting the presence and importance of this particular pattern, it is still reasonable to attribute it to learned cultural behavior. This is clear when we note the contrasts in the training of males and females in our society and the differential frequency of violent acts performed by them as adults. Boys learn aggressiveness because it is "manly," and girls learn to avoid it for the same reason. A small boy in our society at the threshold of awareness of living things is not innately violent. He has empathy with fireflies, sowbugs, spiders, and earthworms. When he kills his first small bird with a stone or B-B gun, the feeling is more likely to be one of sadness and shame than of "manly" accomplishment.

Cooperation serves as the desirable alternative to aggression and violence. On the international level, at which reactions are most critical for all peoples, we may point first to the one institution which attempts to speak for all mankind, the United Nations. Despite its failings, it is still the organization which most nearly represents the ideals of humanness. It is likely to have a difficult time surviving if only because it is an acephalous organization with little power to implement its prime purpose, to support the rights of man. Functioning more smoothly are the international monetary organizations and business combines which draw resources from diverse nations and are controlled by representatives of several nations. Admittedly, these organizations are hesitant and often falter, but their achievements in international cooperation, although limited to date, are hopeful augers for the future. International tensions may be reduced significantly in years to come through cultural exchange programs, the efforts of the Peace Corps and similar organizations, and international travel in general. Each of these endeavors fosters understanding of other peoples and brings with it the realization that people around the world are in their essence one and that survival of one's own population depends directly on the respect and understanding accorded other societies.

6

FAMILY LIFE

To be able to single out one major configuration of human social behavior as universal would make anthropologists feel that they had a solid base from which to project man's social future. Until recently it appeared that the nuclear or conjugal family, composed of a man, his wife, and their children, was irreplaceable as the basic unit of social organization. Although families created as the result of plural marriages are rather common around the world, these seem basically to be a special form of the nuclear unit. From a polygynous marriage, in which a man marries two or more women, more than one nuclear family results. Polyandry, in which two or more men marry one woman, is much rarer but has been authenticated in a few areas of the world. It produces a nuclear family with two or more heads. Another variation is the extended family, a larger unit composed of individuals closely related through a parent-child base. This type of family might, for example, consist of a man, his wife, their sons, and the sons' wives and children. In this type of family a nuclear family forms the organizational core. The nuclear family is the entirety of a monogamous family, the essence of the polygamous families, and the unit base of an extended family. Thus, the nuclear family often has been identified as the key, nonreducible social unit basic to all small- and large-scale societies.

A cluster of complementary reasons have been advanced in order to explain the universality of the nuclear family. First, the nuclear family setting offers stable and sustained sexual gratification to the adult male and female members. This factor alone becomes a strong binding force between the two most critical members of the unit. Some societies also permit or encourage sexual intercourse outside of marriage, but all societies approve of it first and foremost between a husband and wife. Second, a cohabiting man and woman are the reproductive foundation from which the society is perpetuated. A third binding force is the complementary nature of the economic activities of men and women. The sexual division of labor reported to a greater or lesser extent for all societies becomes the sound basis for male-female partnership. A husband is the provider of food and protection, whereas his wife is the preparer of food and the one most often responsible for routine child care. It might be noted too that pregnant females and those with infants or young children cannot normally be self-sufficient. A fourth quality of the nuclear family is that it provides the simplest organizational unit possible for teaching children many cultural and social norms. Here children may efficiently learn much of what will later be expected from them; boys learn the most from their fathers and girls from their mothers. Thus, the most fundamental needs of a society are open to fulfillment by a simple but durable dyadic relationship between a man and woman.

Although the nuclear family was viewed as universal, it was realized that other social institutions might supplement its functions. For example, nonfamilial guilds might assume the responsibility for training children in craft skills; village elders might play an active role in educating children, and nuclear family subsistence welfare might be subordinated to control by a larger economic group. It would seem from this that all of the nuclear family obligations could be satisfied by a group of other interlocking institutions, but no ongoing society, either primitive or complex, had been accepted as having sustained such a social system over a period of generations. Exceptions do exist which have been differentially interpreted, and it is instructive to consider three of the most significant. If one or more viable societies can be found in which the nuclear family is not a basic unit, then its essential nature may be questioned.

A SOVIET EXPERIMENT Following the revolution of 1917, a purposeful effort was made by the leaders of the Soviet Union to destroy the traditional form of the Russian family along with its supporting institutions. After the Soviet leaders had consolidated their power, they made a concerted effort to create a new and totally unprecedented sociocultural system. In order to do this, they decided that the Greek Catholic Russian Orthodox Church dogma and extended family customs must be negated. In pre-revolutionary Russia the patriarchal family and the Orthodox Church had been linked in a number of key institutional patterns. Matrimonial negotiations, marriages, divorces, and family life were social and also religious concerns; furthermore, a man had almost complete legal control over his wife. The Soviet leaders implemented a series of radical changes designed to destroy these customs. Church weddings were ruled illegal; in order to marry, the couple simply registered with a local board, with no ritual involved. Prior to 1917 divorces were difficult to obtain, but shortly thereafter a couple could receive a divorce simply by applying for it. Either spouse could make the application, and the court was obligated to grant it. The nonconsenting partner, if absent from the proceedings, was notified of the court's decision by postcard. In 1920, as a part of the continuing effort to grant women freedom and equality comparable to that of men, a woman could obtain an abortion at a state hospital without justifying her request on any grounds. These policies were accompanied by an abolition of inheritances and a refusal to distinguish between legitimate and illegitimate offspring. By 1927 common-law marriages were given legal recognition. Children were taught in the schools that their first obligations were to the state rather than to their parents, and they were encouraged to report any anti-Soviet views of their parents to their teachers. The state had reserved the right to assign a man and his wife to jobs in different sectors of the Soviet Union, and there was no appeal from these separations.

By the early 1930s the nature of family life had been altered drastically, but the Soviet planners were forced to reassess their policies because of certain unanticipated results. During 1934 only 57,000 infants were born in Moscow, whereas in the same year 154,000 abortions were performed in the city. Furthermore, during this same year there were thirty-seven divorces for each one hundred marriages, another factor tending to depress the birthrate. By 1937 the Soviet population had fallen some thirteen million persons behind the normal anticipated ratio of increase. It also became apparent that because of family instability and undermined familial authority, juvenile delinquency had increased at an alarming rate. Newspapers reported property destruction by youthful gangs, beatings of teachers, sadistic crimes, and murders. Some women, perhaps even most young women, appreciated their newfound freedom, but others considered that the Bolshevik policies had ruined their lives. A man might marry a woman, live with her for a few days or weeks, and then divorce her, repeating the process as often as he chose. In order to correct this abuse of the system new policies were implemented in 1934. Marriage now was stated to be "the most serious affair in life," and marital unions were expected to be lifelong. Family stability was praised, and it became increasingly difficult to obtain a divorce. A man who married one day and obtained a divorce the next was charged with rape. By 1936 divorce proceedings had been made expensive, and the cost increased with each divorce. Furthermore, both parties were required to be present at the hearings, and reconciliations were attempted. By 1944 the divorce laws had become even more stringent, and it was necessary to satisfy the courts that serious attempts at reconciliation had failed before a divorce was granted. The proceedings were carried through two levels of the courts and were very expensive. In 1935 an anti-abortion campaign was launched, and by the next year it was possible to obtain an abortion only if it could be demonstrated that the woman's health was endangered by the pregnancy. In 1935 also, a propaganda campaign was begun to restore parental authority, and laws were enacted to curb juvenile delinquency.

A retrospective evaluation of the Soviet program to destroy traditional family life was made in 1950–1951. Life histories were obtained from persons who had been parents or children in the Soviet Union during the early post-revolutionary period but who had moved to Germany or New York City. The refugees interviewed may not be considered a true cross-section of Russian citizens; in fact, their attitudes toward the Soviet authorities most often were hostile. Despite the bias of the sample, however, certain inferences may be derived from an analysis of their life histories. Those persons who had been parents of small children during the early period of Soviet rule usually disliked the Soviet policies, but they had not spoken out against them at the beginning for fear their children would inform on them. The parent-child relationship had been altered successfully by the state largely because the immature children could be indoctrinated by the state before they could be reasoned with by their parents. After a child was twelve to sixteen years of age and subject to reason, most parents expressed their distrust of the state policies, but their views of hostility most often were rejected by the child. One of the major conclusions to be drawn is that the Soviet planners succeeded in instilling the values of the state in the children even though these ran counter to the ideals which prevailed in most families. Since the state agents began their indoctrination program when the children still were very young, and since they took action against any parents reported as hostile by their children, the parents felt helpless in guiding their own children's attitudes during their formative years. By the time a child had reached an age of reason, the attitudes of the state were firmly entrenched in his mind. These older children, by bringing social pressures to bear on their parents, further forced parental conformity to the aims of the Soviets.

Although the Soviet indoctrination methods proved to be highly successful, the policy revisions of 1934 indicate that the new family instability had created some undesirable social conditions. This led to a partial return to former concepts about the ideal form of family structure. Although the powerful extended family remained defunct, the nuclear family reassumed a more stable form after the experimental era.

THE NAYAR NOVELTY The Soviet example of forced social change which partially succeeded bears comparison with an instance in which long-term forces at work in a society gradually produced an extraordinary form of familial organization. The people involved are the Nayar, who lived along the Malabar coast of southwestern India. When the British began their local control in 1792, the Nayar men were professional soldiers who were away from their homes for at least a part of each year either fighting or training for warfare. Nayar social life was organized around a system of castes and subcastes, with memberships ranging from royalty to commoners. Villagers considered themselves related through females (matrilineal descent) and from four to seven female kin groups (matrilineages) in a village comprised a subcaste of commoners. Through the matrilineages, property ownership passed down a direct female line. Females and matrilineally related males comprised household groups who tilled or leased lands which they held jointly. The household head was the eldest male who lived permanently with the women and children. Within a village linked matrilineages of commoners served primarily as guardians of morality, and they organized the prepuberty "marriage" rituals. A male took a "wife" from within his subcaste and from a linked matrilineage. Every few years prepubescent girls were ritually married to men selected by the village astrologer. The couple was isolated for three days, and the man left after the fourth day. After this time the man had no further obligations to the girl, and the "bride" had no duties toward the man except to observe certain customs at the time of his death. The marriage rite, called *tali* after the name of the gold ornament presented to the bride by the groom, elevated the girl to adult status. Shortly before or soon after her menarche she might begin having sexual intercourse with her "husband," with any man that stood in the same social position to her as her husband, or with any man in a higher subcaste or caste. The husband had no special claim to his wife and was able to have sexual relations with her only if she were willing. A woman might have from about three to eight habitual sexual partners, and she might change to new ones whenever she chose. When a man and woman agreed to have sexual relations, the man visited the woman's house and left his weapons outside the door to her room, thus serving notice to any man who arrived later that she was occupied for the night. Given these general conditions, it is not surprising that the paternity of an offspring might be uncertain or unknown. The one or more men who claimed paternity of an infant paid a delivery fee to the midwife; this was the only obligation of fatherhood. The children were cared for by the mother and members of her household, and a child called its mother's current man "lord." A woman and a man, either her husband or some other male, might grow fond of each other and sleep together frequently. Under these circumstances, the man involved presented the woman with gifts of luxury items, but still he did not support her, her children by him, or her household. One social force operated to discourage a man from becoming deeply attached to a particular woman: the man's relatives distrusted these emotional involvements because they feared that he might give the woman gifts and money which were rightfully theirs; thus they made every effort to break off any relationship which seemed to be assuming stability.

In the tradition of Nayar social life, the critical characteristics of family organization do not occur within a nuclear setting. A man and his wife did not form a coresidence unit, a father was not responsible for the economic welfare of his wife or offspring, and he did not contribute to the socialization of his children. Furthermore, a man was likely to have his primary sexual relations with women other than his wife.

DYADS AND DADS Anthropologists often are said to be obsessed with possible exceptions, and my descriptions of Soviet and Nayar family life are in this tradition. At the same time exceptions, even partial exceptions, to any rule are important, for they make it possible to legitimately question the universality of the rule. If there is one valid example of a society which did not have the nuclear family as the basis for its social system, as is true of the Nayar, then we must be prepared to question the indispensability of the nuclear family as the basis for human social life. In addition, the Soviet example illustrates that many of the functions usually attributed to the family can be replaced with at least partial success by other institutional forms. The nuclear family is widespread, dominant, and virtually universal, but at the same time its existence is not incommutable but rather is based on man-made decisions. Even if we had not found the exceptions, we logically would expect them to occur if only because any form of family organization is socially, not genetically, derived.

Since the nuclear family is almost basic and almost universal, it is not surprising that it embraces those social units which are both basic and universal. The most fundamental social relationships are dyadic or paired, and the most essential dyad is the male and female sex partnership. It is the agreement to have sexual intercourse and the sexual involvement itself that produces the sexual dyad. Only copulation, between clean sheets or otherwise, can lead to the conception which is vital to perpetuation of the species. Most often the sexual dyad is expressed through the social convention of marriage, but marriage is by no means essential for this dyadic relationship. The second fundamental dyad is a direct result of the first; when a woman gives birth to an offspring, a maternal dyad has been created. During the prenatal and postnatal development a functional dependency binds the offspring to its mother or to a wet nurse who becomes a mother substitute. It is a physiological bond, with the mother's ability to provide nourishment and care as the vital base. The sexual dyad and the maternal dyad together provide the social and biological links between generations. A third basic dyad is that which exists between offspring of the same mother. Although it serves no vital function, this dyad exists universally simply because a mother most often bears more than one child and these offspring are united through their common upbringing by her.

The fourth paired relationship, which may or may not be present, is paternal, between a father and child, and it is qualitatively different from all of the others. It exists largely because the sexual dyad led to aftereffects, an offspring. The paternal dyad has no essential biological function, but it may be extremely important in sociocultural terms. A male is necessary in order to impregnate a female, but this does not lead to an inherent need for the male to continue his association with the female. The fertile female is the key to the entire biosocial system, whereas the male who has fertilized her may or may not assume a stable relationship with her before or after an offspring is produced. In the nuclear family and in the basic dyadic relationships, the female-mother is critical. The father retains his associations with the child only if his role is so defined by the norms of the society. Although a father may have a lasting interest in his children, they are not bound to him physiologically at any time, and therefore his presence is not essential to them.

In some areas of the world the maternal dyad is the most basic social unit for significant portions of the population. When a family is organized around a woman and her children as the stable members, it may be termed matricentered or matrifocal. This form is widespread in Latin America. In Nicaragua and El Salvador, for example, a quarter of all households are matricentered. However, not all matricentered households are composed of matrifocal families. Some, although probably not many, households would consist of a woman alone or a woman with dependent parents, siblings, or others. The matrifocal family should not be viewed as a phenomenon among exotic peoples alone. Of the forty-five million families in the United States in 1960, twenty-five million were nuclear families, and four million of these were matricentered. Two million of these female-headed families included children under eighteen years of age.

The matricentered family is best described in a 1951–1952 study of a village in British Guiana fictitiously called August Town. The matricentered families of August Town represented thirty-seven percent of the two hundred and fifty households. A mother guided the destiny of her household. If a husband-father was present, he became the legal household head but tended to be peripheral to the actual functioning of the household. A household was formed when a man and woman legally married or assumed a common-law marital relationship. In lower-class households common-law marriages were favored; this reflected the couple's reluctance to commit themselves to more permanent marital arrangements. Soon after the cohabitation, the woman bore an offspring; at that time she depended on a man for economic support and was under his direct authority. A man's continued status in a household depended on how much he contributed to the support of his dependents. This town had a color scale, and the blacker a man's skin the less chance he had of being steadily employed. A woman did some gardening to support her household, and she became increasingly free from dependence on a father-husband as her sons matured and were able to contribute to the support of the family. One of the key reasons an attached male was not important in the rearing of children was that as an unskilled worker he could teach his sons little which would aid them in the economic system. Life in the households of such British Guiana Negroes was and is bleak and fraught with economic insecurity. Depressing as this social system appears to be, it is nonetheless important to note that the matricentered household is, in this cultural setting, a successful adjustment to economic and social realities.

MOTHERS AND CHILDREN The preceding presentation of family life indicates that the social relationship most essential to the continuance of societies is that between a mother and her child or children. By briefly exploring this relationship in a cross-cultural perspective it becomes possible to establish the impact of the major variables which seem to determine the nature of the mother-child dyad. *Mothers of Six Cultures* by Leigh Minturn and William W. Lambert (1964) is the most thoughtful comparative study on the topic. The six peoples studied in 1954–1955 lived in widely separated areas of the world. One of the six cultures was a segment of "Orchard Town," a New England community of 1000 people in an area which rapidly was becoming suburban. The second study site was a village barrio in the Oaxacan town of Juxtlahuaca, Mexico, with a Mixtec Indian population of six hundred persons. Tarong, a barrio studied in the Philippines on the northwest coast of Luzon, was occupied by nearly three hundred persons, whereas the study site of Taira on Okinawa had some seven hundred persons. The village of Khalapur in Uttar Pradesh, India, had a population of 5000, of whom 2000 belonged to the Rajput caste which was selected for analysis. The Gusii, a Bantu-speaking tribe in Kenya, were represented by about two hundred persons clustered in a densely populated area.

The comparisons made of these societies concentrated on the variables confronting mothers in them and how these affected the socialization of the children. The mother-child relationships varied more within a society than between societies, and yet it was possible to characterize prevailing patterns in each separate society. For example, maternal warmth was scaled according to general warmth, general hostility, the amount of praise a mother used, and the frequency as well as the intensity of the punishment which she brought to bear on her children. Although the differences in these characteristics from one society to the next were not great, it was found that the mothers in Mexico and India offered their children the least warmth. The authors hypothesized that maternal warmth was determined largely by household living conditions. The Mexican and Indian families lived in courtyard or courtyard-like households with other children and other mothers in their midst. Where greater privacy existed, as in the African and Philippine households, there was more maternal warmth, and it was even greater among the Okinawan mothers, who had still more privacy. However, the New England women, with their almost cloistered privacy, were not the warmest mothers, perhaps because their physical isolation with only their children was so extreme that it was emotionally oppressive. In terms of maternal instability, on scales of mood variations of hostility and warmth, the Gusii and New England mothers were the most unstable. In both instances the emotional instability appears to have resulted from the fact that only the mothers were available to care for their children for extended periods. It also seems that women who have significant economic obligations in addition to child rearing duties are more demanding in terms of responsibility training and also punish more severely.

This very brief discussion of the attitudes of mothers toward their children may seem obtuse in terms of our society, and yet there are cross-cultural lessons to be learned. One is simply that working mothers, of necessity, consider first their economic responsibilities and then their children. Such mothers are both more efficient and less permissive with an offspring. As this indicates, many child rearing practices stem not from ideals concerning how children should be raised but from a host of very real social and cultural factors which impinge on the daily life of a mother. The size of the household, the number of children, familial duties, and economic obligations of a mother establish the manner in which she will deal with her children.

FAMILY LIFE IN THE UNITED STATES   Social life in the United States today is organized around economically independent nuclear families who occupy separate dwellings. Each newly married couple seeks a residence separate from the parents of either spouse, a marriage residence pattern termed neolocal. This pattern may be contrasted with that of a few generations ago, when the population was less mobile and was concentrated in rural America. Life among families of farmers in the past focused on the land holdings of the father. A man's children were raised on his farm, and when the sons married they brought their wives into their parents' home; daughters married the sons of nearby farmers and joined their households. The sons' families might have overcrowded the original family dwelling, in which case they built new houses nearby. The sons continued to till the land of their father and hopefully were able to purchase additional farmland nearby. After the death of the father, his sons either divided the land or tilled it in common. If sons were left landless, they migrated to a frontier and acquired land on their own or else joined an urban population. Settled farm life took place in an extended family setting, and marital residence was patrilocal, based on a continuity of land occupation by a direct line of males. More recently the pattern has shifted away from large, extended families living in a rural setting to small, nuclear families in an urban environment as the most important social, economic, and residential units.

In an effort to sustain continuity with the past we idealize the extended family group as it formerly existed. The nostalgic attitudes of parents or grandparents about the advantages of rural life are familiar to many of us. These reminiscences stress the simple desires and ambitions of their generation, their common-sense approach to problems, and the leisurely pace to their lives. Life on the farm, however, is not remembered as easy, for there was hard work, deprivation, and a constant struggle against the elements. Events which today attempt to reunite the extended group include family reunions, weddings, and funerals of its members. At the same time, any effort to expand an urban family residence unit to include parents or grandparents as permanent members is likely to be resisted by the adult members of the nuclear group. Old people are thought to belong in rest homes and retirement communities where they can find happiness in the midst of other old folks who share common interests. The social and economic importance of the extended family as it formerly existed now is largely a part of our cultural heritage. We may even note more recent changes in family life which have brought distinct alterations in our nuclear family style of living. The increasing divorce rate, number of husband-wife separations, and the physical mobility of families are more often deplored than applauded. The question often is asked, "Where will it all end?"—the answer is very clear and quite simple, "With man."

Perhaps in the recent past the nuclear family was relatively independent, tightly integrated, and free to chart its own course according to the abilities and inclinations of the adult members, but these conditions, if they ever existed in fact, no longer prevail. Nuclear family obligations are currently often neglected or even abrogated in many ways. A father may abandon his family socially and economically (desert), socially but not economically (pay support), psychologically (his job, sports, intoxicants, and so on), or in a combination of ways. When all of these possibilities for a father's abandonment are totaled, the effect on the society can be inferred. Within the nuclear family unit, situations leading to a reformulation of role responsibilities have become increasingly common. The emergence of social surrogates is a significant pattern of our time. Even those parents who consider themselves as providing familial stability delegate their responsibility for the development of their children to baby-sitters; to teachers of nursery schools, kindergartens, public schools, and boarding schools; to leaders of Camp Fire Girls or Cub Scouts, and to summer camps, to mention only the most common substitutes. This abdication of traditionally parental obligations to the representatives of other social institutions is an inevitable consequence of our social ways and of the need for children to be trained to live in our complex society. Because children must learn so much that is beyond the instructional capabilities or inclination of most parents, an offspring at the age of six, or even earlier, must necessarily be taught by the society at large. The dwelling in which a family resides is the base from which its members operate, but this has tended increasingly to become a house rather than a home. The members, except perhaps the wife and infants, go forth each day to jobs and schools, and the older members often go off again in the evening in search of additional training or entertainment. Many a house has become a place in which to sleep and sometimes to eat, but life is "lived" beyond its walls.

The continuation of the nuclear family as a viable unit in our society seems to depend on its success in satisfying the primary and secondary drives of its members. During a period of rapid change such as the current one, the basic social unit must remain extremely flexible in order to survive, which in turn calls for a virtual abandonment of the traditional ideas about the nature of life both in the nuclear and extended family setting. Of the primary needs, the one fulfilled most satisfactorily between the adults of a nuclear family is that of sex. It is difficult to obtain undercover information on the incidence of adultery, but a safe conservative statistic is that half of the men and a quarter of the women in lasting marriages have at least sampled such sexual relations. Nonetheless, the majority of sexual activity still occurs within the marriage bonds. In a worldwide sample of societies, we find that the vast majority of peoples disapprove of adultery; a few peoples provisionally permit it, and only a small minority openly sanction it. Thus, with respect to this aspect of marital sex life, our society fits well into the worldly pattern.

In spite of the increasing incidence of nonlegitimate progeny in our society, which reflects the increased separation between the sexual and the paternal dyads, the nuclear family continues to be the main reproductive unit leading to our biological continuity. The clear potential exists, however, for the sexual dyad and the follow-up of a maternal dyad to become the norm in some society, perhaps even our own. Even these conditions may in time give way to test-tube babies, and the normal mother-offspring relationship may be replaced by nonfamilial institutions charged with child rearing.

The third criterion on which nuclear family organization has been based, the complementary nature of the economic functions of a man and woman, clearly is changing its character in our society. The socially defined division of labor is no longer rigid, and comparatively few job opportunities are now limited to one sex or the other. Although women are seldom employed as carpenters, plumbers, or laborers, partially because these activities are controlled largely by powerful labor unions, these few remaining divisions of labor tend to be based somewhat on physical distinctions. Thus, go-go girls far outnumber go-go guys—at least presently. By and large, however, the job tasks which can be filled by a man are within a woman's capabilities. The expansion of women into traditionally nonwomanly fields such as airline pilots, engineers, bus drivers, and uniformed police suggests a shift in our attitudes concerning jobs and sex.

The changes in what is fitting male or female work reflect an altered pattern of statuses, the positions which individuals may occupy. In small-scale societies virtually every man was a husband, father, and hunter, whereas each woman was a wife, mother, preparer of food, and rearer of children. In all societies, simple or complex, certain statuses are ascribed to each person because of his sex (male or female), age (infant, child, adult, and so on), and kinship ties (son, daughter, uncle, aunt, and so on); other ascribed statuses may reflect class or inherited social position (a peasant, king, slave, princess, and so on). One distinctive characteristic of complex societies is the diversity of statuses which are achieved, not ascribed. Variations in individual roles begin to appear in those tribal societies in which one man might become a shaman by learning the necessary skills, while another makes bows, trades, or specializes in fishing. In tribal societies most statuses are ascribed, however, and each person tends to fit into a rigid social order, few alternatives being possible despite any individual initiative. Rigidity of ascribed statuses also tends to eliminate competition, and tradition guides individuals into established roles. In settings such as these it is possible to anticipate one's social future rather clearly. In more complex societies achieved statuses become extremely important. These are realized through the mastery of skills and are most often gained through competition among individuals striving within a socially flexible environment. A great diversity of such achieved statuses characterizes our society at the present time. For example, through training and ability a sales clerk may become a store owner, a merchandise buyer, a personnel director, or an advertising director. What is further notable among us is the opening of once exclusively male-achieved statuses to females on the basis of proven ability alone. This general trend is clearly a threat to the balanced economic roles of males and females formerly found both within and beyond the boundaries of the nuclear family and makes economic interdependence less significant as a binder to hold males and females together.

The fourth and final characteristic of the nuclear family is its important position in teaching children the norms of the sociocultural system in which they are being reared. In this regard, the point already has been made that parents have largely relegated their children to an assortment of institutions in our society which are responsible for specific phases of child rearing. This replacement is not necessarily desired by parents; it is rather a by-product of the increasing complexity of our society, which leads to an acknowledgment by parents that they are unable to fill all the enculturative roles.

When the four key criteria of nuclear family organization are evaluated together in terms of our lives today, it must be admitted that the unit has lost some of its former pertinence. In general terms, there is nothing socially pathological about the family instability in our society; it simply represents one adjustment to our changing world. In most instances, it might be noted, divorce is followed by the formation of new nuclear families rather than the replacement of this unit with some other form. One major cross-cultural study of divorce sampled forty non-European societies from all of the major regions of the world and from the various levels of cultural complexity. One society, the Crow Indians of the American Plains, encouraged divorces, and a man was ridiculed if he kept any particular wife for very long. Apart from this extreme example, it was found that in terms of marriage stability, sixty percent of the societies had divorce rates which exceeded our present rate. In none of these societies is there any suggestion of social pathology because of the incidence of divorce. It also might be noted that in thirty of the forty societies there was no great difference between the rights of men and women to initiate a divorce.

If we consider the Nayar, we realize that the nuclear family is not essential for the perpetuation of a society. The British Guiana Negro inhabitants of August Town further demonstrate that a major segment of a society may continue to function outside of what is considered usual in terms of family structure. In a like vein about a quarter of the Negro families in the United States are matricentered, probably for many of the same reasons that gave rise to the situation in British Guiana. The Soviet effort to change the nature of family organization was not entirely successful in spite of the power and purpose of the planners. This example illustrates, however, that governmental intervention into the nature of family structure may so drastically alter previous norms that there can be no possible return to previous patterns. In this context we may note the growing liberalization of divorce laws in the United States as well as the Supreme Court decision that a husbandless woman receiving Aid to Dependent Children for her offspring cannot be deprived of support simply because there is a "man in the house." These are examples of governmental response to needs becoming increasingly definitive as the traditional structure of family life in the United States has changed.

In sum, the stability of the nuclear family is lessening in the United States today, and the functions of the nuclear family are being delegated—voluntarily or otherwise—to other institutions. As a result, one of our major needs in social planning might be toward strengthening the position of husbandless mothers. It already has been established that the mother-child relationship is the most basic and lasting dyad in any society because of the long-term dependency of an offspring. The material analyzed in *Mothers of Six Cultures* indicates the way in which this relationship is affected by the economic as well as social position of the mother. Formal and informal efforts may need to be directed toward providing greater emotional and economic support for women who raise their children to the point at which the society as a whole can assume the greater burden of responsibilities. I do not suggest that we plan and legislate against the nuclear family, but rather that we do not neglect the primary and secondary needs of mothers without husbands and children without fathers.

7

AMERICAN KINSHIP

If anthropologists have a true love, it probably is for the kinship systems of tribal peoples. For over a hundred years and with singular diligence, long lists of the kinship terms employed by different peoples have been recorded. An inordinate amount of time and energy has been devoted to this task, and the compilations occasionally have been an end in themselves. More often, however, ethnographers have reasoned that by assembling kinship terms and analyzing their linguistic and social meanings, we gain great insight into the ways in which people view relatives, the group of person most likely to influence an individual's life. A knowledge of the terminology used for relatives suggests the manner in which one behaves toward them and thus permits entry into the essence of a people's social thoughts and actions. Relatives may be defined as those persons to whom we consider ourselves joined through the ties of blood or marriage. To us they are "family," "folks," "kin," "kith and kin," "kinfolk," "my people," or "relatives." Certain words are used to differentiate one relationship from another, and we behave toward each category of relatives in an accepted manner without giving the matter much thought. Because we think of relatives in terms of our kinship system, we quite reasonably tend to assume that our designations and patterns of behavior are shared by most other peoples around the world. This assumption, however, is not justified; our general pattern for distinguishing kinsmen is just one of eleven reasonably common systemic possibilities, within which there are hundreds of variations. It is helpful to consider a contrasting type of kinship system, for only in this manner may we come to understand the significance of the patterning within our own system.

It may reasonably be suggested but cannot be proved that kinship terms, along with all other patterns in human behavior, evolved. Before there were words for relatives, the early man-apes no doubt had feelings of closeness with other man-apes in their group, and these thoughts would in time find expression as distinct sound combinations with definite meanings. The abstraction "people," originated to distinguish one's habitual companions from "enemies," possibly was an early step in the expression of band consciousness. As more refined distinctions between individuals within one's own band evolved, the male-female and old-young differences possibly were among the first status contrasts categorized. A simple and highly operational, although not necessarily the earliest, set of kin terms might be conceived as follows. A person would group all males on his father's generational level under a single term. At the same time he would have a different term for all females of his mother's general age group. A reasonable extension of this pattern would be to have another word apply to all males of his own generation and to employ a still different word for all females in this age group. Finally, there might be a reciprocal term which the young applied to the very old and vice versa. A general system such as this is one of the simplest operational means to designate persons within one's own group. The differences would be thought of in terms of sexual and generational distinctions, which are contrasts drawn by most peoples even today. The core of this system, which is one of the eleven major kinship patterns, is to terminologically group mother, mother's sister, and father's sister while employing another term for father, father's brother, and mother's brother. This subsystem grouping for the ascending generation above ego is called generational. When the term for brother is extended to male parallel cousins (father's brothers' or mother's sisters' male children) and to male cross-cousins (father's sisters' or mother's brothers' male children) while the term for sister is extended to female parallel and cross-cousins, the sibling-cousin terminology is called Hawaiian. If a people has bilateral descent (meaning that essentially equal stress is given to recognition of relatives on both sides of the family), Hawaiian cousin terms, and a generational terminology for the first generation above ego, the type of social structure is labeled "Hawaiian." This system, intact or with slight variations, is very common around the world and has been reported among such diverse peoples as the Ifugao of the Philippines, the Kaingang of Brazil, and the Maori of New Zealand. In any interpretation of the system it is quite obvious that thinking of parents' brothers and sisters as "mother" and "father" and applying the words for sister and brother to all cousins, leads to much greater feelings of closeness with these sets of individuals than does the very different set of terms in our society.

It should not be supposed that members of a tribal society with kin designations of the form just described are unaware of biological paternity when they lump "father" with "uncle" or male "cousin" with "brother." The biological nature of procreation probably was known to all of the world's primitive peoples when they first met Euro-Americans, although there may be a few exceptions to this statement. In any event, the word a people might use for father-uncle does not imply biological paternity as does the word "father" to us. Furthermore, they could distinguish between father and uncle if called on to do so. It is simply that they do not consider the difference between them to be important normally, and therefore the separation is not made.

Our own particular system of social organization, based primarily on our kinship terminology, is termed "Eskimo," and it will be discussed shortly. The Hawaiian, Eskimo, Yuman, Fox, and the seven other most common systems are each differentiated by words used for certain categories of relatives as well as accompanying rules for tracing one's descent. Each system is conceptually quite distinct, which has led to contrasting means for classifying relatives. The reader interested in further details about the diverse forms of kinship terminologies should consult the bibliographic sources for this chapter.

SOCIAL NORMS Before considering our own kinship terms with their accompanying behavioral expectations, it is helpful to consider certain aspects of social organization in general so that we may better understand the broad context in which kin terms are employed. Around the world there are certain universal social dimensions to living which are implemented through customary or legal norms. All peoples have rules to distinguish relatives from nonrelatives and established ways in which to trace patterns of relationships or to define whom one may or may not marry. Likewise, the possible number of spouses, the location of a newly married couple's residence, and the inheritors of property are established by the social standards of a people. These matters, along with the terms and behaviors characterizing relatives, become the core of social customs.

In the United States we trace our relatives along both our father's and mother's blood lines, and therefore our descent system is termed bilateral. This norm is not at first obvious since family names are carried solely by the male line, and because we are patronymic, it is mentally easier for us to think of our father's relatives. If we were asked to list all our relatives, however, we would include both the paternal and maternal lines. We do not consistently feel a great deal closer to one side of our family than to the other. We visit persons on both sides and receive them as guests, we inherit wealth along both lines, and we probably do not consciously consider paternal uncles, aunts, or cousins as any more or less closely related to us than the same individuals on our mother's side of the family. These statements are true for the population as a whole, and yet a particular individual may feel closer ties with his father's or his mother's side of the family because of their geographical proximity, wealth, or attitudes of affection and warmth.

One important characteristic of our bilateral descent system is that only you and your biological brothers and sisters, siblings, have precisely the same set of blood relatives, that is, the same personal kindred. The individuals to whom you are able to trace direct known blood ties are your kin. In some families this network of relatives is not remembered beyond grandparents and grandchildren, whereas in other families the ties may be traceable to great-great-grandparents, great-aunts, second cousins (first cousins once removed), and so on, depending on the happenstance of family wealth, births, marriages, and deaths as well as individual and family efforts to maintain, record, or remember such bonds. The social focus of an adult is on his family of procreation and perhaps on his siblings within generally a rather narrow circle of relatives.

Contrasting our system of kin designations with a form which differs only slightly will convey something about the largely unique position in which each of us finds himself with reference to his relatives. If we traced our relatives only through males (that is, along a patrilineal line), our ties would be primarily with the persons bearing our family name, and we could plot such relationships step by step, thereby creating a patrilineage. Included in a male's patrilineage would be his paternal grandfather; his father; his father's brothers and their sons; himself, and his sons, as well as closely related unmarried females who retained the family name. If the family name were Smith, then all the related Smiths would form an ongoing unit or corporate group, and the fact that your name was Smith would integrate you firmly into the group, permitting comparatively little accommodation for your personal feelings toward any individual in that group. Of course there would be many other persons named Smith with whom you would be unable to trace kinship ties. If you felt that these Smiths were related to you, you would number them among members of your patrisib even though you were unable to trace person-to-person ties. Thus, all the Smiths would be distinct from all of the Joneses and Taylors; each would have its own patrilineage and patrisib.

As our bilateral system works out, persons with several different family names may be members of one's personal kindred, and we divide our feelings of loyalty among a number of name groups. The greatest strains are placed on our kindred system in crisis situations: when inheritance pricks our greed, when personal animosities occurring within the limits of our kinship group require us to take sides, or perhaps when an unlikable relative arrives at the front door with a mountain of luggage. These are instances in which we might prefer to define our kinship duties with precision and to limit kinship obligations to a single lineage. At the same time, when feelings within a kindred are harmonious, we profit emotionally and materialistically. We might borrow money from a mother's sister, spend a summer with a father's brother, seek and receive advice from a mother's brother, take a father's sister's child under our protection, and so on.

The matter of inheriting money and property, or even keepsakes, poses innumerable problems in our society, partially because of our kindred organization. A "rich uncle" who is a bachelor and has several "poor nieces and nephews" illustrates the point. The uncle may be a man's or a woman's brother, and he may feel himself equally close to all the children of his siblings. To whom he should leave his legacy is a problem not resolved by any set of rules or laws. Thus, the potential heirs may vie with one another for the uncle's attention, thereby hoping to profit materially at the time of his death. If, however, our society were strongly oriented toward the paternal line, the man's brother's children would routinely reap material gain with their uncle's death.

Our marriage laws are precise and prohibit us from having more than one spouse at any one time, which leads to our monogamous state. Our particular form of monogamy is somewhat distinctive but not unheard of elsewhere in the world. We have serial or sequential monogamy, which means that while we are permitted only one spouse at a time we may, with considerable ease, replace the first with a second and so on.

As mentioned previously, we tend to set up residential units after marriage which are physically and economically independent of the households of our parents or parents-in-law. One of the primary effects of this residence norm is to decrease or negate the ties between parents and their adult children and to remove the effective influence of grandparents in the training of grandchildren.

OUR KINSHIP TERMS One of the first observations about our kin terminology is that the words used for relatives vary with the circumstances surrounding their use. Among the more important considerations in selecting a term is whether the relative is spoken to directly or is talked about, and if he is talked about, the person spoken to may be important. Thus, there are terms of direct address and terms of reference, and the latter may be altered according to who the listener may be. A boy may address his father as "dad"; he may refer to the same individual as "father" when speaking to his mother and call him "the old man" when talking to his sister. The sex of the listener is another variable which is sometimes important; a boy who refers to his father as "the old man" when speaking to his sister may refer to him as "the old bastard" to a male agemate. The use of possessive pronouns is another means for adding clarity and precision when employing reference terms, for example, "my father." In a like manner the sex of the speaker may be important; a boy who refers to his father as "dad" may have a sister who consistently uses "daddy" in the same context. In addition, we recognize that the terms used may change with the age of the individual speaking or being referred to. A small child may call his mother "mamma," as an adolescent may shift to the word "mom," and may feel most comfortable saying "mother" when he is an adult. Certain words which designate relatives are almost always used as terms of reference; these include husband, wife, or first cousin once removed. Whether other terms are used for address only, for reference only, or in either set of circumstances, may differ from one family to the next even within similar subcultural backgrounds. We also may note that use of certain terms will vary with the socioeconomic background of the individual employing them.

The following list of kin terms, used either for address or reference, is not exhaustive, but it does indicate the terminological variability for father and mother.

Father	Mother
dad	ma
daddio	mamma
daddums	ma'am
daddy	mammy
father	mom
pa	mommy
papa	mum
pappy	mother
pop	mumsy

Within the nuclear family the terms used to address one's father and mother vary widely. Although most of the differences are slight variations on the words "dad" and "papa" or "mama" and "mom," these changes may be significant indicators of the nature of the emotional ties involved. When a grown daughter addresses her father as "dad," the connotation is not the same as if she said "daddio," and both of these words carry a far different meaning than does "father." Likewise a son who calls his mother "mom" reflects a different attitude toward her than if he were to use the word "mother." What is notable about the alternative words for father and mother is not only the numerousness of the variations, but also the shade of meaning which each conveys. The word "father" as a term of address or reference carries the full recognition of male parental dominance. Thus, for a child habitually to call his father "dad" or "daddy" suggests that the male referred to neither demands nor receives full paternal respect. On the other hand, some older males avoid using any kinship term at all when addressing their fathers during an argument, the implication being that in such a context any word for father carries the association of authority. This deliberate avoidance of using a kin term is a "zero" designation. It appears further that the use of a single term for father is rare. If the form most commonly used is "father," we find that the alternative is likely to be "dad"; a person using the term "pa" would most easily use "pop" alternately. If these observations are correct, a man cannot be both a "father" and a "pop" to his child.

It is not uncommon for children to range beyond the list of kinship terms for parents in order to find others which are admissible alternatives. A father might be called by such nonkin terms as "governor," "master," "pater," "sire," or "sir"; at present these are most likely to be caustic terms of address or reference. In a historical context, each of these substitute terms for father, and to a lesser degree the word "father" itself, implies the subordination of the child. One obvious reason that these words have passed out of common usage is that children no longer are as fully subordinated to their fathers as they were in the not-too-distant past.

The social ties which bind a child to his mother differ somewhat from those between a father and a child; the word "mother" does not carry with it a meaning of dominance equal to that of "father." For example, when arguing with his mother, a male might very well use the term "mother" even though he would refrain from using "father" in the same context. Neither are there nonkin terms of authority, currently used critically, for mothers, with the possible exception of "ma'am." A son is likely to use the word "mom" or "ma" whereas his sister uses "mother," which again suggests that a mother is regarded differently by sons than she is by daughters.

A further terminological possibility is for a child to use his father's or mother's first name when speaking either to or about them. The everyday use of parents' given names by children is increasingly common and represents a new type of egalitarianism which contrasts most strikingly with the former usage of authoritarian, nonkin terms. A final mixed category of father-mother terms includes diminutives, nicknames, designations carried over from childhood, and idiosyncratic family-specific names.

The paucity of kin terms for son and daughter offers a rather striking contrast with the numerous variations for father and mother. Children are most often addressed and referred to by their given names; this may be because of terminological confusion resulting from having one or several individuals in this category, although there also is the possibility that parents are attempting to deal with their offspring in an essentially egalitarian manner. Both parents and children are well aware, however, that parents, because of their age, maturation, and social status, have implicit control over their children. The nearest approach to parent-child terminological equality occurs when members of each set address those in the other by their given names. Parents do not usually address their children as "son" and "daughter," and although there is the alternative kin term "sonny" for a boy, there is no other common kin term for a girl except the displaced term "sister." Sons and daughters may be designated as "boys" and "girls" collectively or by words such as diminutives, nicknames, and so on. Between siblings, first names are the rule, but variations in direct address terms include "bud" or "buddy" for "brother" and "sis" or "sissy" for sister.

The final category of nuclear family terms includes those employed between a husband and wife. Probably few men today habitually address their wives as "wife," and the same would apply to a woman's use of the word "husband," although both words are common as referential terms. The spouse's given name, or some variation of it, is used most often in direct address. Thus, the bonds of marriage leading to the husband-wife set are expressed in a very limited kinship terminology. Some people in fact maintain that a husband or wife is not truly a relative as are their other kin. A spouse is a key individual in the procreation set, and the unique nature of a husband-wife relationship is expressed most cogently in terms denoting an intimate relationship. An infinite number of idiosyncratic designations for a spouse exist although they may never be known to anyone except the couple involved. Examples of such wife terms are "stinky" or "sloppy floppy all butt," and husband designations of the same order include "big ears" and "hairy." In addition to given names and highly personal terms for a spouse, there exists a broad category of commonly accepted terms denoting intimacy. Husbands, as well as boyfriends and lovers who are potential husbands, may be designated by such animal terms as "tiger" or "bear," and less often as "dog" or "wolf." Animal terms for a wife include "kitten" and "bunny" with "bitch" as not inadmissible. Wives also may respond to bird designations such as "pigeon" and "dove" or the vegetable names of "tomato" or "pumpkin." Mutual terms of affection include "darling," "dear," "honey," "love," "sugar," and "sweetie." Displaced kin terms also are employed, as when a husband calls his wife "mother" or a wife terms her husband as "father." Usually the rationale for these designations is to teach young children the proper kin terms, but the usage may continue between spouses after the children are grown up or may even occur between partners in a childless marriage. Even though most words for a spouse are outside the accepted list of kin terms, in absolute number and in diversity the possible word alternatives are unequaled elsewhere in our kinship system. This great variety is understandable in light of the individualistic nature of each marital set. Romantic love with all of its shades of meaning, the highly unique social experiences in each person's life, and the happenstance of finding a person to love, all are conditions which contribute to the different ways in which a husband and wife address and refer to each other.

Variations on uncle and aunt terms include the uncommon appela-tions "unc" and "auntie," but these individuals are much more often referred to or addressed as "uncle" or "aunt," by one of these terms plus a first name, or by first name alone. Just as with siblings and offspring, the uncle or aunt relationship may apply to more than one person. If this occurs in the first two sets, the tendency is for the given name to be used in address or referral. This is not always true in the uncle-aunt category however. Uncles and aunts bear two types of relationship since they include not only the siblings of one's parents but the in-marrying spouses of these siblings. Since an in-marrying uncle or aunt does not generally appear to be terminologically distinguished from one in a blood line, this factor does not form a naming distinction. It does appear, however, that some persons are likely to use first names alone for uncles but not for aunts, or they may use an aunt's first name if she is on the mother's side of the family. An aunt on the father's side of a family is more likely to be called by the kin term or the kin term plus a first name. Uncle or aunt terms sometimes are employed early in a child's life but dropped as the child grows up. Most notable with respect to uncle-aunt designations is the variability of terms depending on personal feelings toward different individuals in these categories. Some persons address a well-liked uncle by his first name because they desire to identify with him, and yet they also may term a disliked uncle by his first name. In the latter case the kin term is avoided in an attempt to pretend that the relationship does not exist. When the word "uncle" plus a first name is used by the same informants, the implication is that the relationship is bland or neutral.

The word "cousin," without any modifier, is a kinship term of reference for most of us, although in the southeastern United States it is an accepted term of address when combined with an individual's name, that is, "Hello, cousin John." First cousins, the children of a parent's sibling, usually are the only individuals thought of as cousins. Cousin is the first kin term thus far encountered which does not distinguish the sex of the individual involved. The fact that we are unable to establish the sex of a cousin by the kin term suggests that such individuals are relatively unimportant in our lives. Except as a term of reference we seldom employ the word cousin; we are most likely to address such individuals by their given names. Furthermore, considerable confusion enters our thinking when we expand beyond the realm of "first cousin." For example, is a "second cousin" a first cousin's child, or is he a "first cousin" of one's parents? What is perhaps important is the fact that we do not agree among ourselves, which is a good indication of our lack of concern with cousins beyond the range of "first cousin."

Another characteristic of our terminology is the use of kin terms for certain individuals who are unrelated to us by ties of either blood or marriage. The most notable of the fictive kin are those unrelated persons who are socially close to one's parents and are termed "aunt" or "uncle" by children. The practice of young children calling an elderly female babysitter "grandmother" is another example of this custom.

Other extensions of kinship terms are made to certain classes of unrelated persons. Reference to church functionaries as "father," "sister," or "brother" are examples. Other members of certain congregations also are sometimes called "brother" or "sister." In a like manner, we may address or refer to an elderly person as "grandfather" or "grandmother." In these cases the kin term indicates a kindly or respectful attitude. We also extend kin terms to more abstract notions in referring to "mother nature" or to God as a "father." The idea of "Uncle Sam" is in the same vein, and some people remind us that Uncle Sam has the role of an "uncle," not that of a "father." In such instances our nonrelated status is clear, and confusions tend to be rare. It is doubtful, for example, that a "red hot mamma" would often be confused with one's own mother or that an individual addressed as a "sugar daddy" would be conceived of as the biological father of the female employing the term.

Anyone who has read the foregoing discussion of kin terms with attentiveness should be able to cite additional kin designations or meanings which differ somewhat from those presented. Each of us thinks about relatives sooner or later, and we may cast our thoughts about them into words in various ways. We may employ the "standard," nationally accepted terms, use unique familial or individual words, reflect regional terminology, or choose among alternative terms which may or may not reflect geographic or socioeconomic distinctions. One favorite truism in ethnography is, "Some people do and others don't." Nowhere is this observation more obviously true than with reference to our kinship behavior. For example, some persons greet a relative, no matter how distant the tie, with a kiss as an acknowledgment of the relationship. In the southern United States individuals who greet each other in this way are "kissin' cousins." Although the term is widely known outside of the South, it is unlikely that most persons could define the nature of this relationship or the range of persons to whom it is applied. The variability in designations for relatives may be illustrated with yet another type of example. The terms that a woman may use to address her husband's father include "father," "father" plus his last name, "father" plus his first name, his first name alone, "Mr." plus his last name, or literally no name at all. Once again, those persons who employ different terms of address have accepted slightly different role relationships.

Informants asked to list our kinship terms would give the standard or normative terms such as "father," "mother," "son," "daughter," and so on. Only later would the alternative terms such as "dad," "pop," or "mom" be cited. Furthermore, the range of application for some standard terms brings forth feelings of ambiguity. Whether or not a cousin's husband or wife is considered a relative varies with the informant. In addition, some persons may use the normative terms quite differently, as when a wife is called "mother." The terms usually are not considered in the context of "right" or "wrong," but as variations acceptable for ourselves or other persons. Thus, our ideal pattern with its precise terms is a guide which accommodates many variations.

Our basic kinship structure has been offered without recourse to its ramifications or to a discussion of the more technical details. In technical terms our system is "Eskimo" because we have a bilateral descent system, "Eskimo" cousin terms (cross and parallel cousins are not distinguished from each other but are distinguished from siblings), and lineal terms for the first ascending generation above ego. (Father is distinguished from father's brother and mother's brother, but the latter are terminologically equated with each other. The same pattern exists for females at this generational level.) It should be apparent that one characteristic of our system is that the nuclear family is the basic unit. Beyond the nuclear family our custom is to lump relatives into broad or classificatory units. Among some other peoples, fatherlike or brotherlike terms are extended to include uncles and cousins, and among them the nuclear family would not have the same social meaning as among ourselves. In a society in which the term "father" refers also to father's brothers, father's sister's husband, and all the males of their generation, the kinship structure is very different from our own. In this case "father" really conveys the idea of "men in my father's generation." Such a system provides a very broad protective network of social relations. We on the other hand isolate the nuclear family, and in so doing we seem to say, "Nuclear family, stand or fall on your own."

Within the nuclear family we have noted considerable variability in the range of acceptable kin designations for father and mother, which does not seem out of the ordinary because it is our accepted pattern. It is unlikely that we would find comparable terminological latitude anywhere in the ethnographic literature. Eskimos, for example, have a single word that means father, and while it may be mispronounced by infants and children, this word alone is the one applied by anyone to a male parent. The same is true of nearly all other Eskimo kinship terms, and a similar lack of variability is reported for most of the world's peoples.

Both within the nuclear family and beyond it we have shown an increasing tendency to set aside kin terms and to address or refer to relatives by their given names. When it is accepted for children to address their parents by their first names, an increasingly common practice, we obviously are moving in an unprecedented social direction. It does not seem farfetched to suggest that we are phasing our kinship terminology out of existence. This projected development becomes all the more reasonable when we consider that our society is increasingly based solely on the nuclear family and that this unit has an inherently unstable membership because of the death or divorce of parents. In addition, we often become geographically separated from siblings, parents, aunts and uncles, as well as first cousins, to provide further barriers for the maintenance of close social ties. Often we cannot even trace our bonds beyond our immediate family unless famous individuals are involved. In fact, if close relatives, even siblings, are underachievers in socioeconomic terms, we tend to ignore their existence.

An important implication of these remarks is to note the increasing tendency for each person to merge as an individual recognized first and foremost by his given and family name; he is no longer thought of primarily as the representative of a particular kinship status. This trend is fully in keeping with our ideal of personal social mobility. An ideal in our society is that each of us achieves according to his abilities, regardless of whether he happens to come from a rich or a poor family background. Today we tend to think of the struggle for the rights of the individual in our society as a new social surge of the 1960s, but this is not the case. We have idealized these rights ever since we became a distinct national entity, and our kin terms have undergone a gradual adaptation to this concept. The rights of the individual have been reflected in our gradually changed behaviors toward both near and distant relatives and have come to be projected beyond the range of relatives to the society as a whole.

One hypothesis which may account for our adaptations is that changes in social structure are initiated through shifts in marriage residence patterns and that these in turn will lead eventually to changes in other dimensions of social life, including kinship behaviors and terms. It appears that our shift in marital residence from colonial and more recent patrilocality to current neolocality has brought an accompanying shift from extended family to nuclear family orientation. As the nuclear unit becomes less stable, we appear to be developing more individually oriented behavior. The individual, with his own rights and responsibilities, is beginning to emerge as the basic unit of our social structure.

8

THE CITY

If time, nature, and nurture joined through culture to make man into anything, it was to create the world's most successful hunter. Not so very long ago most men subsisted primarily by killing wild animals for food. No cities or towns existed then, for life was lived within a band, as a member of a hamlet, or in a village. Life among hunters and their families is difficult for us today to comprehend, let alone appreciate, and yet the economic foundation of most societies until some 10,000 years ago was hunting. In these societies it rarely was possible to maintain large numbers of persons at any particular time or place. Hunters and those who depended on them often were hungry and sometimes starved; social security then was a by-product of the kindness of others when it existed at all. As difficult as it might have been for such persons to thrive, or at times even to survive, there was a nobility in their manner of living. They knew the ways of the natural world and took much of its patterning for their own. To stalk an animal required skill, persistence, and patience, each with its dramatic tensions. The kill might be exhausting, exciting, and danger-ous, but it was at the same time directly rewarding. The feeling of personal accomplishment attained by outwitting and destroying the earth's other animals in order to eat was psychically satisfying just as the resultant meal was gastrically fulfilling. The ancestors of all men were hunters at one time or another, and even in our current affluence we may look back with admiration on their resourcefulness.

Although I feel an admiration for ancient and contemporary hunting peoples, I recognize the value of the more certain paths to survival which replaced hunting economies many years ago. One early form of more stable subsistence was shellfish collection. To gather shellfish at low tide required little time and no imagination, but the harvest, supplemented with animals and plants from the sea, provided a rather reliable if uninspiring economic base. Much the same may be said of the economies of many fishermen around the world. The subsistence certainties and relative stability of fishermen and collectors are only slight, however, when compared with the economic security and growth potential made possibly by the advent of farming.

THE FIRST FARMERS It is customary, almost obligatory, for anthropologists to note that when man first domesticated plants he precipitated a cultural "revolution." I offer this traditional observation but cannot bring myself to believe that it was entirely a step forward. Instead, I tend to think that the development of intensified farming economies was the most unkind trick that culture ever has played on man. As hunters, individual men exercised a remarkable degree of direct control over their futures. That they required cultural devices is not questioned, but their cultural forms were uncomplicated extensions of themselves; the hunter and his ways blended into the natural setting. Each day of his adult life a man realized his successes or failures; thus he was at least a partial master of his own fate. However, when men began to farm intensively for a living, they created an unnatural landscape of cultivated fields. Then cities arose as even more bizarre environmental modifications. Like the hunter, the farmer and city dweller are at times driven by the elements and the vicissitudes of nature, but in addition, farmers and urbanites are so deeply involved in the complexities of their cultural systems that they are in a very real sense enslaved by an artificial environment built more by accident than by design.

The first seeds heralding the "revolution" sprouted in the Near East about 10,000 years ago, probably in the area ranging from Israel to southern Turkey, eastern Iraq, and western Iran. Here, along a crescent that was extremely fertile there lived peoples whose economies were based on the collection of foods as well as the hunting of animals. Among the plant products gathered were forms of barley, lentils, peas, and wheat. The region likewise supported populations of wild asses, cattle, dogs, goats, horses, and pigs. The technological products of these Near Easterners included stone-bladed sickles for cutting wild grasses as well as milling stones and mullers to pulverize seeds. On the well-watered uplands, at elevations between two and four thousand feet above sea level, wild grasses grew abundantly. The most important of these were wheat, which grew only along the hilly flanks of the crescent, and barley, which was common over a much wider area. In their natural habitat the grains of wild barley and wheat drop from the seed spikes after they have fully ripened, and they are scattered by the winds. It was essential to harvest these grasses just before the seeds dispersed. How it came to pass that the barley and wheat seeds harvested one year came to be sown the following year is unknown. Perhaps seeds accidentally were dropped on a garbage pile and sprouted the next year to produce a small but rich crop, which suggested the idea of purposeful planting to someone. In any event, by 7000 B.C. in eastern Iraq, domestic crops of barley and wheat were sown and harvested. A distinct genetic quality of the early domestic forms was that the ripened seeds remained encased in the seed spikes rather than falling to the ground. Such plants grew in the wild but were few since they did not propagate themselves effectively. However, these were precisely the genetic strains that had the greatest harvest potential for man, and because they depended on man for their effective propagation, they became the earliest known cultigens. Wheat and barley were planted at elevations lower than their natural habitat, and man no doubt learned to select the moisture-laden planting sites which were most likely to yield large harvests.

In this setting also were a group of wild animals which had greater potential as domestics than any collection of diverse species found together elsewhere in the world. The dog probably was the second animal domesticated by man, if we accept the proposition that the first was woman—who still might best be classed as in a semidomestic state. The second, or third, domestic animal was the goat, which initially was raised for its meat. Perhaps goats were first kept as pets, and their potential as a ready source of food may have been realized at this time. How goats first became tolerant of man may only be speculated. One possibility is that a newborn goat was discovered shortly after birth and that it thought "mother" when it saw a human. The baby goat may have been taken home and raised by a nursing woman in the finder's family. She may have nursed two kids at once and raised the goat in the household. Goats, and later sheep, cattle, and pigs, only became true domestics when they were successfully bred by man and assumed physical characteristics different from those of their wild cousins.

At the small settlement of Jarmo in eastern Iraq, archeologists have uncovered the remains of an early group of sedentary farmers. These people lived about 7000 B.C. in a community consisting of about twenty-five rectangular, mud-walled houses which were occupied throughout the year. Their domestic grains, barley and wheat, were supplemented by lentils, peas, and vetchling; these possibly were collected from wild plants. The people also gathered acorns, pistachio nuts, and snails for food. Dogs and goats were domestic animals, and perhaps the same was true of sheep. The other local animals were wild and were hunted. Quite obviously the economic base was broad, the diet was balanced, and food sources were reasonably dependable. It has been estimated that the average population of Jarmo was one hundred and fifty and that the site possibly was occupied for around three hundred years. The subsistence base reported at Jarmo probably was that of incipient farmers, a type found over much of the Near East at this time period. Around 5000 B.C. people with this way of life began to wander into the alluvial lowlands of the Tigris and Euphrates river systems. Here they settled as bottomland farmers who continued to raise barley and wheat as their primary staples but added cultivated dates to their diet as well as fish from the lowland waters. Before long, the flat, alluvial farmlands were laced with canal systems designed to irrigate the plots of land needed in the expanding cultivation. The natural warmth of the area coupled with an abundant water supply and wild plants which could be productively cultivated served to carry food production far beyond anything ever before realized. This combination of conditions was critical in the emergence of a radically new form of social setting, the city. The cultural achievements necessary before large aggregates of persons could gather in cities included the establishment of a farming economy which produced dependable food surpluses year after year, the development of an effective means to store these surpluses, and the establishment of a collecting and redistributing system for the products reaped.

THE FIRST CITIES   The word city, derived from *civitas*, referred to either an administrative or ecclesiastical district in the time of the Roman Empire. The rise of cities, the earliest being in old Mesopotamia, is the second "revolution" proclaimed by most anthropologists. By 4000 B.C. many changes were beginning to take place in Mesopotamia and adjacent areas, and cities were emerging which had both of the definitional qualities of cities set forth by the Romans. The core of a Mesopotamian city and the area adjoining it formed an administrative unit or city-state inhabited in some instances by tens of thousands of persons. The city-states were great experimental centers in which human labors became sharply differentiated. Quite possibly the earliest and most important force integrating city dwellers was religious. Great temples with cult chambers, workshops, and storage facilities were constructed. The men in charge of these building complexes were fulltime specialists in religious matters and were possibly the earliest priestly group. They not only were responsible for rites and rituals, but they also assumed secular or bureaucratic responsibilities. Religious and administrative functions seem to have been combined in the earliest city-states, but before very long there was an emergence of hereditary secular leaders or kings, whose palaces began to rival the temples in grandeur. In addition to being administrative and religious centers, the early cities were the *loci* of great markets, which served as the hub for far-reaching trading activities.

In this new environment social differences developed among men, and these soon introduced radical changes in human behavior. The manner of living for priests and kings was vastly different from that of the landless city-dweller or the village farmer. There also developed classes of artisans, traders, merchants, and lesser functionaries in the religious and bureaucratic systems. The class structure of human society crystallized in the city to produce great social distinctions which separated the rich from the poor—the haves from the have-nots —and human living lost its egalitarian quality.

TYPES OF CITIES   Between a city, no matter where it is, and a village or hamlet of any tribal society, we have a play of opposites, and yet no two cities themselves are identical. In an ordering of cities three major types with striking contrasts among them have been identified. The first type, the traditional city, is one which sustains an old and long-established civilization. These cities probably arose when a local tribal base expanded into a local folk tradition. The city emerged as a center from which a city-state developed, and the latter was crystallized finally as a nation. These cities are the great centers of learning, and they carry forward a homogeneous cultural tradition by sustaining and preserving the richness of a great civilization. Few such cities exist today; perhaps the best examples are Peking, Lhasa, and Kyoto.

A second type of city includes those which arose to fulfill commercial needs. Although some are old, they are not ancient, nor were they ever great centers of traditional learning. They are the great market and trading centers of the world, and in them persons of divergent backgrounds are drawn together. New York, London, Marseilles, and Shanghai represent this type.

The third major category is that of cities which arose primarily as administrative centers. Examples would include Washington, D.C., New Delhi, Canberra, and many of the state capitals in the United States. Life in a commercial or administrative city contrasts in purpose and in pace with that of a city of tradition. Commercial and administrative cities are heterogeneous in their population composition and in their subcultural diversity. In these environments no great traditions prevail; on the contrary, it is here that dissent and heresies emerge and flourish. With their atmosphere of nonconformity, they seem to invite individualistic ways among their inhabitants.

This classification of cities into three types may be further refined to distinguish subtypes, but to do so would bring no new perspective to the present discussion. In order to contrast the qualities of cities, two which are very different in their form and history will be described. The first is Timbuctoo, a trading center which emerged and flourished outside the sphere of Western cities. The second has been termed the "ultimate city" by one writer and the "city of the future" by many others; it is of course Los Angeles, the City of Angels.

TIMBUCTOO This city is as appealing to anthropologists as it is to others interested in faraway places with exotic names. Fortunately, we know a great deal about the people of Timbuctoo because of a field study in 1940 by Horace Miner. He was attracted there because Timbuctoo was a primitive city which emerged from a Moslem, rather than European or American, cultural background. Thus it provided a testing ground for defining the nature of city living outside the context of Western civilization. The city, or perhaps more justly the town, since it had only about 6000 residents in 1940, is located near the area where the jungle meets the desert in west Africa on the great northern bend of the Niger River. The first historical reference to it was made around A.D. 1000 when it was discussed in Arabic records. The location was first a camp for herders of the southern Sahara Desert, but as Arab penetration of the area intensified, it was here that a great commercial center arose to link the north and south. The city passed in and out of Arabic and local control, but it always served as a great market for Arabs from the north, the local Songhoi and Taureg, and various peoples from the south. European and Arabic trade goods from regions beyond the Sahara and slabs of rock salt mined in the central Sahara were transshipped through Timbuctoo to the Sudan, where they were exchanged for gold, slaves, and ivory. The residents of Timbuctoo were obsessed with keeping Europeans away from their city, and as a result French control was not effected until 1893. Raids against caravans by desert nomads continued until the 1930s, indicating the unwillingness of the local populace to succumb to foreign domination.

In 1940 the city core was composed of one- or two-story, rectangular, mud houses with flat roofs supported by wood beams and covered with thatch and dirt. Buttressed doorways broke the walls facing the winding streets, and the city was divided roughly into quarters. Persons of similar ethnic background tended to live in each section. The centrally-located marketplace was the city hub, and two mosques were the only additional landmarks of note. The people of the city represented diverse linguistic and cultural backgrounds. A large block of the population was composed of Arabs with a mixed Negro and Caucasian or a Caucasian genetic background. The Arabs in the city were urban merchants; those who lived nearby were desert nomads, often referred to as Moors. With the Arabs were their Negroid slaves derived from West Africa. A majority of the population was composed of Songhoi, who spoke a Sudanese language. They were divided into a serf group called Gabibi, who were predominantly Negro and originated from the Sudan, and another group, the Arma, who were descendants of sixteenth century Moroccan Arab men and Sudanese women. Nearby the Caucasoid Taureg, who were desert nomads, dominated the mixed blood Daga, also desert pastoralists. The town-dwelling Bela were Negroid slaves to the Taureg. Physical appearance usually was a poor means for distinguishing one population segment from another in Timbuctoo, but the people may have been separated ethnically on the basis of clothing, hair styles, and adornments.

Timbuctoo existed because of its importance as a commercial center. The market was the heart of this city which drew life from the people who lived there because of business involvements or who came there to trade. The merchants, traders, transporters, and producers each had a single goal—to gain monetarily as much as possible in each transaction. Buying and selling was impersonal, cold, and calculated, largely because the persons involved were very ethnocentric and the accumulation of wealth was the wholehearted goal of all. The ideals of honesty and fair play in commercial matters were known to all, but these guidelines were recalled and defended only by the loser in a transaction. To cheat a stranger of all his goods was commendable as long as one was not caught, to attenuate a product before selling it was routine, to hold back an honest return from an employer was institutionalized, and dishonest weights and measures were so ordinary that they were "standardized." It is little wonder that a unified civil government never emerged from within the city and resulted only from conquest by outsiders. Neither is it strange that the people of Timbuctoo never joined to defend themselves against invaders or that the market routine continued no matter who the rulers might have been at the moment.

In the value system family and ethnic cohesion was important in life-crisis involvements, economic pursuits, religious behavior, place of residence, and language. Beyond these integrative networks, however, it remained possible for a person to strike out on his own economically and to succeed or fail as an individual. Thus the economic environment tended to draw the individual away from his family, friends, and others of his ethnic identity. Admittedly, the aid of friends and relatives was sought but primarily in order to further personal aspirations. What an individual could not gain through labor, luck, and family help, he might obtain by theft, which was individualized and extremely common. The ideal of familial and ethnic cohesion clearly conflicted with individual aspirations, and the resultant stresses and strains on individuals and groups found expression in diverse ways. For example, a hockey game played between males of rival quarters provided simultaneously a strong reinforcement of ethnic identity and a violent release of stresses.

Timbuctoo in 1940 stood nearer the ideal of a small-scale integrated society than to the complex, modern cities with which we are familiar. Furthermore, because it is a foreign city, it has a cultural background which is strange to us as are the peoples represented there. Nonetheless, several aspects of living in Timbuctoo find parallels among ourselves. The stress of individual achievement, wealth and money; the incidence of crime; the impersonal nature of business life, and the obvious cheating as well as the hidden dishonesties all appear to be a part of city life wherever the emphasis is on commercial activities.

LOS ANGELES Among cities Los Angeles is in a class unto itself, a fact which many people admit freely, with some fervently adding "Amen." It did not originate as a center for either traditional learning or governmental administration. Although its size has forced it to become a commercial center of increasing importance, it did not emerge as a crossroad for trading activities. Why then did Los Angeles become a city, and what does its emergence suggest with respect to urban living?

In 1781 the pueblo of Los Angeles was founded as an agricultural settlement by the Spanish. They had recruited a small group of settlers in Mexico, and these individuals were given land as well as livestock and farming equipment. By 1800 the agricultural productivity of Los Angeles was exceeded in California only by that of the San Gabriel mission. An overland trade route to Santa Fe, New Mexico, was opened by 1830, and before long the Monroe Doctrine, manifest destiny, and a vague realization of the potential of California made the area attractive to expansionists in the United States. Mexican control of California was fragile, and the Mexican War, together with the Bear Flag Revolt shortly before, enabled the United States to gain California through military action by early 1847. In the 1850s Los Angeles was a rough-and-ready cow town where fights, murders, and lynchings were common events. Until the late 1860s the economy of southern California was based largely on great cattle ranches, but droughts brought a gradual shift to small farms. By 1870 Los Angeles contained nearly six thousand persons; in terms of city population it ranked 139th in the United States, whereas San Francisco was ninth.

The tempo of local life began to change in the 1870s with the founding of banks, the opening of a woolen mill, the increased production of wine, and the entry of an overland railroad. The initial impact of the railroad was not great, due to the excessively high rates of the Southern Pacific and its selection of a relatively isolated route. Only when a competing line, the Santa Fe, completed its service to Los Angeles late in 1885, was there a remarkable change in the City of Angels. Before the Santa Fe Railroad drove its last spike, the passenger rate between the Mississippi Valley and southern California was about $125. When cutthroat competition began on March 5, 1886, the fare between Chicago and Los Angeles dropped to $32; later the same day it was reduced to $25. The next day Kansas City to Los Angeles fare began at $12, and before noon it was $10. Within a few weeks the rates stabilized, and for about a year the fare from stations along the Missouri River to Los Angeles was $25. The immediate effect of the rate war was to bring a veritable flood of people into Los Angeles. The population of 11,000 soon increased to 80,000, and through the railroad competition, the fabulous boom of the 1880s began. Before this time southern California had been considered a "warm Siberia," but henceforth it was on its way to becoming a cultural center in the western world.

Railroad competition would have meant comparatively little if southern California had been unattractive, but early descriptive accounts by travelers, letters of residents or visitors, railroad and western newspaper propaganda soon disseminated information about the glories of the climate, the fantastic agricultural possibilities, the beauty of the landscape, and investment potentialities of the area. An indication of the rapid increase in property values is seen in the Los Angeles assessment figures of nearly five million in 1880 and forty-five million by 1890. The boom was over by the latter date, but the banks did not fail. Only the paper fortunes of many speculators collapsed. The 1890s saw an expansion of land cultivation, with grapes and citrus fruits becoming increasingly important products. The phenomenal growth of Los Angeles since that time has been most directly attributable to successful advertising of the local climate. Los Angeles was described as the "Garden of Paradise," and migrants came from the other states, from Europe, and from the Far East. By 1900 one-fifth of the population was of alien derivation.

With the discovery of oil in 1893 another important local resource was added to that of good agricultural land in the Los Angeles area. However, the expansion of the city was hampered by the lack of adequate sources of fresh water. The problem was solved temporarily by diverting water from the Owens Valley, in central California, to Los Angeles. In later years additional water was obtained from the Colorado River to satisfy the ever-expanding needs. In the second decade of the nineteenth century the motion picture business began to emerge as important, and within ten years aircraft production was added to the list of prominent local industries.

The development of the pueblo of Los Angeles into a thriving, continuously growing city may be attributed to multiple factors. Although the initial growth of the town into a city was not based solely on the climate, this factor has been very important in the local growth since 1885. Because of the pure, dry air the area was heralded particularly as an ideal setting for those suffering from asthma and tuberculosis. Health seekers, retired persons, investors, tourists, and people seeking a cold-free area in which to winter or to live lent individual and personal impetus to the expansion. The natural resources and the climate also lured the aircraft and motion picture industries to the city. In a sense it is preposterous that one of the world's greatest and most rapidly expanding cities should thrive largely because of its climate. This basis, that of a sunshine center, hardly seems comparable to those intellectual, commercial, or administrative bases underlying the other great cities of the world. A second critical factor in the development of Los Angeles has been its rapid adaptation of technological advances. First, the railroad brought an effective end to isolation from the remainder of the continent. Then the engineering feat of transporting water over long distances to the desert setting permitted vast expansion. The airplane intensified what the railroad had started and expanded the sphere of Los Angeles across the Pacific Ocean. Another technological device, the automobile, made it possible for the city to spread and sprawl. In a broad sense, it is the systemic pattern of transportation technology more than any other cultural aspect that has given rise to the Los Angeles of today.

The very existence of a city such as Los Angeles must be considered a notable cultural achievement of our time. Imaginative Western technology, the mild climate, and American ideas about the "good life" have built this city, and the same combination may well influence the development of many cities in the future. Since these things happened first in Los Angeles, the city has grown up with something of a make-believe quality, a reality that is somehow not quite real. Many established residents and newcomers, both young and old, frantically pursue sun-kissed living. They may choose from a wide variety of microenvironments in which to settle. Included are beach-fronts, palisades, mountains, hillsides, lake shores, canyons, and rolling or flat lands, each with its own further variability. Even poor persons find that the ghettos in this city are "superior" to those in most other urban environments. Its residents number three million persons in the metropolitan area and some six million in the surrounding urban region. No city can rival the current growth rate of the Los Angeles area, with nearly a thousand newcomers each day. Expansion during the early 1960s saw some 260 acres "urbanized" daily. Statistics such as these illustrate a reality that in scope is just barely imaginable. This city which is the technological center for the most sophisticated new industries is at the same time the greatest of make-believe playlands as typified by the ultimates in modern fantasy, Hollywood and Disney-land.

TRIBALITES AND URBANITES We tend to take an urban environment and city living for granted because it is in these settings that most of us spend our lives. The life of a city dweller is vastly different from that of a hunter, fisherman, collector, or even village farmer. To contrast these environments brings a realization of the degree to which the nature of living has changed during the last 6000 years. Before cities arose, the adults in any group shared the same general body of knowledge; the understandings of one man were likely to be shared by all of the others. Dividing lines of knowledge were based primarily on age and sex. Thus there was a rather limited but widely shared body of sociocultural information available to all. Personality differences clearly, or even emphatically, existed, but these contrasts tended to be muted by an established and traditional pattern of living. The members of tribal societies tended to think alike and to express themselves similarly. Furthermore, within a group of primitives physical appearances were similar since all were closely related. The societies of city dwellers could hardly offer a greater contrast.

In a city, knowledge is specialized, and occupational technology is shared only in a general way, even with other persons who are members of the same socioeconomic group. In a city children of poverty or wealth live in very different settings from each other and from that of a child whose parents are moderately rich or poor. In the city an individual's personal qualifications emerge as critical. In these terms, the ascribed status of an individual dominates less than that status which is achieved. In great and lesser cities, diverse languages are likely to be spoken, and even among the speakers of a single language there may be groups with marked vocabulary differences. Likewise, individuals representing diverse racial strains mingle along the streets of a city. The highly specialized role of the individual city dweller contrasts with the lack of economic specialization among tribal peoples. The closeness of kinship and family ties among tribal peoples has been replaced with a remoteness of such ties among city dwellers. The list of differences might be expanded indefinitely, but one other characteristic seems particularly critical. Peoples in tribal societies have deep emotional attachments to the land that they occupy. The locality in which a tribal people live often is thought to be where the world began and where the first people were created; it is where friends and relatives lie buried. For the city dweller such feelings for a plot of land are inconceivable.

Analogies well-drawn or ill-conceived remain analogies, and yet they provide a perspective of considerable value for yet another view of city living. No anthropologist would question the fact that vast cultural differences separated the aboriginal Shoshone Indians of Nevada and the Hopi of Arizona, and in addition, no reputable student of man presently would suggest that the contrasts resulted from the differing intellectual capacities of the Indian tribes involved. Instead, the differences would be explored in terms of the contrastive qualities of the environmental settings and, perhaps equally as important, the different histories and prehistories of the peoples involved. We may think in much the same terms with reference to the most complex and viable urban center in the country, Los Angeles. It is possible to note that within thirteen miles of each other and in broadly similar geographical settings are Beverly Hills, an indepedent city within Los Angeles, and Watts, a suburb of Los Angeles. However, the differences in the cultural background of the people of

Watts and those of Beverly Hills might be considered as great as those between the Shoshone and Hopi Indians. Admittedly, the residents of Watts and Beverly Hills both speak English, but their dialectic distinctions are as great as those which separate some Indians belonging to different tribes. Furthermore, most of the Watts residents are black, and those in Beverly Hills are predominately white, which is a greater racial difference than that existing between any Indian tribes in North America. A white visitor to Watts or a black visitor to Beverly Hills feels much like a tourist traveling to an exotic area in order to catch a glimpse of the "natives" in their natural habitat. In much the same vein, one might tour certain other sections of Los Angeles to see persons with a way of life derived from China, Japan, or Mexico. Even within "white" sections of Los Angeles the persons of Caucasian racial background live quite differently, as could be noted in comparisons of the central city, Van Nuys, or Malibu patterns. What I am suggesting is that in total cultural patterns the differences between Los Angeles population segments are similar to or even greater than those separating some tribes of primitive peoples.

To pursue the same general line but in a different direction, we may note that among hunters the nuclear family prospers or fails depending on the stability and abilities of its adult members; so it is with the same unit in an urban setting. As a lone tribal hunter cautiously negotiates ice floes or dense jungle undergrowth in search of food, the urban commuter, alone and isolated in his subsistence-directed travel, negotiates crowded freeways with subtle gestures of the hand and foot in order to survive. If he is a capable driver with good equipment and knows the routes, he will arrive at the "kill site" on time. If he has great physical abilities or has been trained to a fine point of intellectual or manual specialization, he will succeed in his subsistence quest. As a mother in a tribal society gathers nuts here, roots there, and berries at another place, the urban mother collects her subsistence items from various supermarket shelves or even from different supermarkets. At the end of a day the families in both settings eat an evening meal together. The tribal woman cooks over her campfire as the urban woman does over her stove, or in some cases as the urban male labors over his barbecue. During weekends and often on vacations the urban family ranges far and wide in car or camper searching for a mountain stream, a desert plot, or a wooded glen, where in the midst of hundreds of other families from similar suburban houses surrounded by asphalt and enveloped in smog, they seek enjoyment in the natural world similar to that found daily by tribal man.

9

OUR TOMORROWS

In the preceding chapters, my purpose was fourfold. My broadest goal was to present a cluster of ideas organized to expose those dimensions of anthropological thinking about custom or culture which are most significant in understanding ourselves. In expanding on this base, select topics of historical pertinence were considered, often in contexts which differed from our own. This effort was designed to slightly shake the reader from a perspective based primarily on his own way of life and to encourage a broader view of what it is to be human. My third aim was to present key qualities which make man unique, to speculate on the emergence of fire, human drives, and family life, and then pursue these topics onto empirical grounds. The final goal was to relate these topics either directly or indirectly to conditions among ourselves today. Most of the subject matter is anthropological, meaning that a set of principles, methods, and views has been applied to aid in the interpretation of man and what he does.

The point now has been reached to advance the fifth and final purpose of this book. It is desirable—in fact obligatory—to summarize the data offered earlier and to draw general conclusions from these materials. Anthropologists studying small-scale societies often derive important conclusions, but these convey comparatively little that seems applicable to our lives today. If anthropology is worthy of being accepted as a science, now or in the future, some of its findings should serve us in a positive manner. Understanding ourselves may be intellectual fun, but to be of real value the data should enable us to anticipate trends in our future and to explore alternative adjustment possibilities. My conclusions are offered in the hope that because they represent a studied approach to critical aspects of our world they may be useful in dealing with our tomorrows. I make no pretense that the conclusions are "culture free" and devoid of personal feelings. Since I am a member of our society with its unique form of culture, I share a positive interest in it, and I no doubt have biases of which I am only vaguely aware. Anyone who has read the text to this point has insight into my attitudes and realizes that my presentation has not been fully objective. As an anthropologist, however, I have attempted to stress humanistic and scientific projections about our future.

These remarks about the role of anthropology must not be construed as implying that anthropologists alone are capable of offering guidelines for the future. Their findings should be of greatest value when they are interpreted in the context of all increases in knowledge, whether they are in the social sciences, physical sciences, or technological fields. Anthropological views are critical, however, since they represent a breadth of approach which is more all-inclusive than that of any other academic discipline concerned with man. The time has come when the views of anthropologists are being sought, along with those of geographers, agronomists, public health workers, and others in order to plan integrated programs directed toward goals that imply change in culture. My interest is to facilitate and encourage the utilization of anthropological ideas which may have pertinence within and beyond the campus setting.

BEYOND TRADITIONAL PATTERNS   In the opening chapter, buttons, Santa Claus, and other forms served to introduce the idea of orderliness in human behavior. The concept of pattern was used to present the idea of coherent and logical association between both bits and blocks of human activities. With few explicit references to patterns as such, this same concept was an implicit organizational theme in all the chapters except for the one dealing with biological man, for whom the patterning is of a different order. The usefulness of patterning is clearest for the development of technology, but it also is a satisfactory guide in the presentation of kinship systems, temporal concepts, or family structuring. Furthermore, the concept is helpful in organizing data about the integration of a tribal society. The systemic patterns of no two tribal peoples are alike, and so it is with respect to their cultures as wholes. Thus, cultures, as learned and shared behaviors, are constituted of pattern configurations, and the particular patterns developed within any culture offer a means of analysis for the culture as a whole.

The notion of patterning in culture may be superimposed on the ways of small-scale societies with ease and even with grace. Applied to our complex culture, however, the pattern concept becomes less apparent. In tribal settings, a man was a hunter and a father above all else, and most of what he knew was in its essence shared by all other normal males. Here the commonality of learning led easily and comfortably into the culture patterning. Urban societies have increasingly defied the normally conceived basis of patterned sociocultural behavior. As time has passed, fewer norms are shared and these less often. Although this is accentuated within the city setting, the tendency is not new, nor is its recognition. It began to develop intensively when the earliest cities were founded. Occupational specialization provided the original impetus for the fragmentation of tribal cultures and led to the development of subcultures. The trend for each individual to occupy a very narrow, highly specialized niche has increased steadily. The employment advertisements in newspapers for the aerospace industry, in itself a highly specialized field, do not state the need for an "engineer," which again in itself is a complex specialization, but rather they require design, analysis, or support engineers. It may be demurred that the aerospace industries are hardly representative of the degree of job specialization in American industry as a whole, and yet it appears that this trend also is emerging in other industrial complexes.

When the concept of patterns is applied to simple, small-scale societies and then to complex, large-scale societies, it is hardly remarkable that striking differences are observed. Because these societal types are extremes the homogeneity of patterning among tribal peoples probably is exaggerated; individuals in some such groups unquestionably differ from one another in distinctive ways. Likewise, the increasing negation of patterned behavior among ourselves probably is not as far-reaching as has been implied, for the routine outline of our daily lives is very much the same throughout the country. Thus, the pattern concept remains among us, but its traditional finiteness is gone. Today, behavioral expressions are far more diffuse, the range of tolerances far greater than ever before, and the scope of deviancy much broader. It is not so much that each individual follows a unique course, sharing little with anyone else, but rather that the variety of acceptable alternatives makes patterns so gross as to negate much of their identity and their pertinence.

IDIOLOGY Some among us say "God is dead," and in much the same phraseology I would suggest that "traditional culture is dying rapidly." Culture, in its anthropological sense, was born with human ways. It was nurtured in tribal societies, but began to falter as the first cities thrived. As a welder of group unity, it is losing ground in the great cities of the world, and in these settings it is best considered as a part of history. Culture is learned, shared, and patterned behavior devoid of instinctive or genetic transmission. We see its strengths and failings all around us. To write that the accepted concept of culture is on the wane and is joining the ranks of hand axes, early American buttons, and extended family unity is iconoclastic and seems almost irreverent until we consider the fact that the outgrowth from this narrowing and limiting perspective might be better adapted to man's functioning in a world of increasing specializations.

In cultural terms the United States is a distinct, unique and particular tradition never again to be replicated. As we look inwardly at the country, we recognize that our roots are historically quite shallow. We see regional subcultures traceable to European countries; for example, the English-tradition background is apparent in New England as is the Spanish-Mexican heritage in New Mexico. The United States has been subdivided also by geographical differences or by those resulting from historical developments. The nation has separations in other ways as well, along the lines of rich or poor; Republican or Democrat; Protestant, Roman Catholic, or Jew; old or young; black or white. Although in small communities these distinctions are overridden, most segments are represented in large cities to form distinctive subcultures. Furthermore, the growth of a city is paralleled by growth of particularism in jobs, from the specialized production workers to lawyers and college teachers who deal with highly obtuse subjects. The possible job permutations among city dwellers is limitless.

I am inclined to believe that future anthropological studies among ourselves will expand along one particular line, with a greater emphasis on descriptive and analytical models concerned with individual uniqueness in all its forms. Ideally, the divisions between sociology, psychology, and anthropology would fade away, and a cross-disciplinary approach to individual behavior would result. This is what the "behavioral scientists" of today are attempting. Anthropologists already have been concerned with the individual to some extent, for "culture and personality" studies are well established even though they are marginal within the discipline as a whole. With individual uniqueness as the point of focus the investigation becomes idiological. This word combines "idio," meaning personal or separate, with "ology," meaning a branch of knowledge; the resultant word, "idiology," therefore may be defined as "knowledge of people as individuals." In these terms we might place the traditional and established concepts of culture, enculturation, institution, and status in at least partial limbo. These remarks must not be construed to mean that there is no pattern represented in the behaviors of people in complex societies, but rather that the importance of group characteristics is being superseded by that of individualism.

Conceivably, there is yet another direction in which anthropologists might profitably move in the study of the modern world. Anthropologists cut their intellectual teeth, as dull as they are, on material culture. Ethnographers filled museums with artifacts and the trade journals with descriptions of what they had collected in distant places, but this phase has largely passed into history. Archeologists still stress material culture because it is the very stuff of which their subdiscipline is made. However, anthropologists virtually have ignored the study of the ways in which our manufactures influence our own culture. This is a field in which engineers, technologists, and advertisers lead us we know not where. It is only for rocket voyages beyond the earth, during which adaptations must be made to an environment recognized as different, that those who study cultural man aid the physical scientists and technicians in creating the artifacts necessary to the new surroundings. This is all well and good, but what about the technological products with which we earthlings are forced to live? This question is being posed by people, both ordinary and extraordinary, who ask what have we done to ourselves. Our appliances with their built-in obsolescence, our frantic search for recreation, our acceptance of new hazards created by our fellowman indicate a lack of understanding or concentrated study on this part of our lives. All that I am really asking is whether anthropologists could interpret the human factors in such a way that our material culture might better contribute to the way of life we determine rather than the reverse condition sustaining itself forever.

TIME AS A THING Time has lost its position among us as an abstract ordering system for events and has become reified as an important quality which we attempt to manipulate. It is something that we "find," "gain," "lose," "kill," "save," "spend," but seldom "have." Perhaps the most important end result, a temporary way station, is the manner in which many persons, especially the young among us, have rejected time-oriented considerations. Youth has at least in part cast aside many of the time patterns of the past. Perhaps the ultimate reaction of youth to our respect for time is the drug "trip," which approaches a form of temporal negation. Another change in the traditional temporal and spatial patterning is revealed in the "instant replay" of news from this world or from space. There is hardly a pause between the occurrence of an event thousands of miles away and the appearance of the episode before our eyes on television. It also is necessary to recognize that we have the increasing tendency to express distance in terms of time rather than space. It matters little how many miles separate New York from Los Angeles; the question is how long a time the journey will require by jet aircraft. More commonly, it is not how much distance separates a man from his work but how much time the trip requires.

When time and space are joined in more traditional thoughts of distance, based on hours and days or feet and miles, we have an established set of associative patterns in mind. We consider that tangible objects exist both in time and space with the added quality of context. We value the custom of removing objects from their traditional temporal and spatial associations and making them an out-of-the-ordinary part of our lives. This process began with the founding of the first museums and zoos, but it recently has assumed unprecedented proportions. For example, the removal of London Bridge from England to Lake Havasu City, Arizona, or the permanent docking of the ocean liner *Queen Mary* in Long Beach, California, illustrate the displacement of massive objects from their traditional associations. Perhaps even more striking is the artificial creation of objects or even "lands" to give substance to displaced time-space reality. Disneyland, with its component jungle and frontier lands, serves as an example of this effort. The same transference process is illustrated by exotic foods, ethnic restaurants, or even plastic snow. Here are repeated instances from diverse segments of our culture in which the positionings of time and space have changed although their meaning of old is at least partially retained. In this regard we note again the tendency toward manipulation of time, in this way adding a cosmopolitan and ageless quality to our everyday lives.

VIOLENCE AGAIN   What has been written in the earlier chapters and what follows will matter little if we fail to deal effectively with violence. Therefore, along with a host of other persons, I offer suggestions for avoiding the sustention of this condition among men. Our violence is judged by some to be the expression of a primary drive for self-preservation; even if we may admit this possibility, at least for the sake of argument, we must stress that alternatives to violence do exist and these would fulfill a drive for self-preservation far more effectively on an individual or group level than does violence. There are no alternatives in the fulfillment of bodily functions which are physiological and basic. We must breath oxygen and eliminate wastes in order to remain alive; substitutes can not satisfy these primary drives. Secondary drives, on the other hand, are not so fundamental and may be satisfied in more than one way. Self-preservation seems to fit better here, and the drive-satisfying methods include cooperation, withdrawal, and violence. Since all three conditions are manifest in behaviors termed social, it is imperative to deal with each within this realm. The psychological, legal, economic, or political implications are a less sound base from which to anticipate successful drive-fulfillment. We must, through our knowledge of societies, find ways in which to anticipate crises of self-preservation and prepare to deal adequately with such crises through methods more conducive to survival than violence would be—in other words, to come to grips with potential violence when withdrawal symptoms are originally manifest and to then seek and apply cooperative ways to dispel the crisis before violence arises.

"Everyman" would hesitate long before venturing to attempt an overhaul of his automobile engine and would undertake the repair of a broken television set with great reluctance. He would not be likely to try his own felony case in court, nor would he attempt to direct a motion picture. "Everyman" nonetheless thinks that because he is a man, he knows both the ills and the cures for the critical social dilemmas of our times because, after all, they are only problems of men like himself. We are largely unwilling to admit that the interpretation of social behavior requires as specialized knowledge as does flying a jet aircraft, planning battles in a war, or filling holes in people's teeth. This reluctance is natural enough because we think we see any social situation as simply an enlargement of our personal living, and we consider ourselves capable of articulating our individual solutions. The difficulty is that we usually lack the perspective to be able to consider more than one side of particular situations. We fail to see the broad implications, and our solutions have a self-centered basis. It is, however, encouraging to find that personal problems today are referred to priests, rabbis, social workers, or psychiatrists with less and less hesitancy. We hopefully are beginning to seek and accept the conclusions of highly trained persons, the social scientists, about ourselves, our neighbors, and others. If this beginning is sustained and if it expands to encompass local and national problems, recourse to violence should diminish greatly.

As Alexander H. Leighton expressed so well in 1949, social science is as yet largely untried. We have had some failures as well as some moderate successes, but the era of sufficient knowledge for successful practice is just beginning. The task will remain difficult, however, because the conclusions offered by social scientists often are not subject to proof, the experimental method rarely being open to them. Furthermore, the objective conclusions reached often require changes from the *status quo*, and these are bound to offend some segments of the population. Even the more cautious social scientist may fall into certain traps which will render his research less effective. He may become involved in long-range abstract problems when the need is for suggestions about crises of an immediate concern; the length of time necessary to move from a study formulation to conclusions may be so long that the problem ranges out of hand in the meantime; there is the danger that oversimplification of the conclusions in order to make them understandable to the nonspecialist will decrease their effectiveness; and even among social scientists, a detrimental struggle for personal power may occur. These are but a few of the difficulties confronting the discipline and those working within its network.

Within and between modern nations are deeply rooted differences concerning what is legitimate human behavior; these differences depend on the subcultural and cultural backgrounds of the persons involved and are not readily changed. Through the writings of travelers, anthropologists, and others, or by personal exposure, we now realize that most peoples accept their own ways without acknowledging possible alternatives of belief or action. The great unifying consideration is that we all are numbered among the human species, and the great divider among us is our cultural ways. Although it is true that a group's way of life may be strongly resistant to change, it should be stressed that radical change is not always, or even usually, necessary if a crisis is dealt with quickly and knowingly.

Stresses among men will always exist. They will arise from threats to one's life or to the lives of friends and relatives; an inability to maintain an adequate level of subsistence; forced idleness, isolation, or restriction of one's movements; and discomfort from pain, heat, or cold, to cite some of the most important forms of deprivation. These stresses and the ensuing frustrations are associated mainly with physical conditions. Only slightly less critical in their dimensions are humiliation, shame, the absence of personal dignity, and the sense of futility as sociocultural forms of deprivation. These also will bring forth cooperation, withdrawal, or aggression with its destructive form —violence.

Given the stress conditions cited and an absence of violence, it often is assumed that the people involved are cooperative because they accept, and may even like, their deprived status. This may be thought about a frustrated black in this country who says, in a sense of servitude, "Yes sir" to a white. It is even more common for depressed blacks to be retiring when with whites or to avoid their company as much as possible. These behaviors may in some instances reflect cooperation and acceptance of roles as second class citizens, but much more often they are instances of withdrawal, the creation of a protective wall around one's self. Withdrawal is not acceptance, however, and indicates only a temporary adjustment to a critical situation. The crisis will not be resolved until more personally satisfying solutions, ones which result in acceptable readjustment, are found through aggression or cooperation. The blacks who storm the streets exemplify the aggressive and potentially violent aftermath of an unresolved crisis. The cooperation approach requires human awareness of the needs of others as its prime ingredient.

Most of our undesirable social situations, just as our more favorable ones, are largely products of our cultural background. In our own society there are the oppressed and the oppressors; in the majority of instances, these may bear the further labels of administrators and those administered. Stresses bear down on administrators just as on those whom they administer, and each group reacts to stresses in much the same manner. The major difference, however, is that the administrator has on his side authority and usually the power to sustain his response. When we abstractly consider persons controlling the activities of others, it usually is in terms of superordinate and subordinate roles typified by a foreman and laborer, god and man, father and son. The changes in our culture today are muting the distinctions between these roles; there is less power and authority at the top and less compliance at the bottom. In real terms we realize that the shop foreman must now deal through the union steward in directing the activities of a laborer, while any god seems increasingly remote and insignificant in the affairs of men. For father and son, the tradition of paternal dominance appears to be diminishing with considerable rapidity. The gulf between "rulers" and people is narrowing in those areas outside of long-established bureaucratic frameworks. Given the rigidity of governmental structure it is unlikely that drastic revisions will take place rapidly, but they surely are on their way. Equality between individuals of contrasting statuses begins to appear as a potentially vital social force. If our culture continues to change in this direction, the aims and goals of all people within and beyond a particular segment of it are more likely to be unified in this manner.

The practical meaning of these projections, when they are considered in their interrelationships, is that the primary drives of all men may come to be accepted as the most human of all goal aspirations conceivable. If these can be fulfilled throughout the world, particular cultures may then concentrate on their own secondary drives. Before I wade further into a philosophical morass, two more observations must be made. The first is that I see an increase in the equality with which one person will deal with another in the future. This projects from the more egalitarian ways by which children are raised, which will in turn lead to less rigidity in all hierarchical relationships. The pyramids of authority will tend to be replaced by a rectangular structure with less social distance between the high and low statuses. As this closeness becomes preeminent, the major means of handling stresses before they lead to aggression and violence will be through cooperation. This course becomes more likely as the degree of equality between the persons involved increases. Stresses will be identified on the basis of complaints, and complaints are best conceived of as "gripes." These are the minuscule comments that have normally been missed because of the great distance between the participants. If such complaints are broadly shared, they become the basis for empirical investigation and are among the most reasonable grounds for effective social action.

MOTHERLY FATHERS AND FATHERLY MOTHERS   One lesson which emerges with clarity from cross-cultural studies of social life is that role expectations are arbitrary. In one society we may find that ideally a father behaves toward his children in much the same manner as in our own. In another society it is expected that a father remain a disinterested outsider in rearing his children even though he is married to their mother and lives with her and the children. The mother's brother in this instance serves as a child's disciplinarian, instructor, and emotional "father." The biological father in turn fills a fatherly role for his sister's children. In much the same manner a mother's sister may serve as a "second mother" for a child, whereas among another people a mother and daughter may behave toward each other as would two sisters in our society. Furthermore, it is not unknown for one man to be the "wife" of another, or for a "god" to be a great-great grandfather. Each of these examples illustrates that role behaviors we view as customary may, among other peoples, be very different from those which we consider as normal and ordinary.

Not only is the behavioral patterning of each group of people arbitrary, but such behaviors always reflect greater or lesser adjustments to new circumstances. Among ourselves in the not-too-distant past, one's father was an authoritarian figure who most often was feared as much or more than he was loved. More recently we have come to think of a father as a "dad" or "daddy" who is a confidant and a considerate advisor. At present the tendency to consider a father on a firstname basis suggests that he is increasingly regarded as an equal by his children, and the same type of change may be seen in the mother-child relationship. One of the traditional and nearly universal functions of the family, in its nuclear, extended or other forms, has been to cushion and mediate a child's relationships with persons beyond a circle of relatives. Among ourselves the family circle recently has become so small and its membership so unstable because of separations, divorces, remarriages, and the redistribution of children, that it is far less effective in serving a mediating function. Add to this fact the amount of childhood learning which now takes place beyond the household in nursery and other schools, plus the increasingly egalitarian ways in which children are viewed within a family, and the result is a fostering of individualism from early childhood onward.

In our emerging social environment the limits of conformity are broad, and individuals are potentially capable of filling one of several roles within a family. What we see among ourselves is a rapid change in the nature of family organization. There are no longer strong social reasons why a husband may not function as a wife in meeting the needs of a child or why a wife cannot fill a fatherly role. The skills of both men and women have blended so that the woman can now earn enough to support a family and the man can function as a home manager. Neither is there any implicit reason why a wife or husband can not serve successfully in both parental roles for the children's upbringing, particularly as these roles diminish in extent. It further appears that adaptability to this indicated change would be easiest for those individuals raised in one-parent, or multiple-sequential parent households.

THE CITY FRONTIER Nearly a third of the residents of the United States, some twenty-four million persons, lived in metropolitan areas in 1900; this number increased to one hundred and eleven million in 1960 and included somewhat more than sixty percent of the people. Furthermore, it is projected that by 1980, one hundred and seventy-four million, or seventy percent of the population, will reside in metropolitan areas. At present one compact residential area of New York City has a population density of 380,000 persons per square mile. An urbanite seldom is unaware of his nonnatural, man-made physical surroundings; the crowded freeways, smog, strains of shopping, and noisy neighbors are but a few of the most obvious causes of trauma. We know full-well that the life expectancy of an urbanite is significantly shorter than that of a rural resident. Furthermore, the city dweller's life is likely to be blighted by heart problems, peptic ulcers, or psychiatric disorders that occur much less often among persons living in small towns or on farms.

Few people would deny that there are many adverse aspects of urban living as it functions at present. However, it is hardly strange, new, or unprecedented for men to create cultural forms and social conditions over which they have little long-range control. In making changes man usually is not even vaguely aware of their potential ramifications. Who, in our own times, could have anticipated the dysfunctions of cigarette smoking, automobiles, or insecticides? Who expected the changes in Santa Claus or in the forms of plain, metal buttons? No one, quite obviously, not because there was a lack of order in these changes, but because no person was far-sighted enough to anticipate all of the variables involved with their direct and indirect side effects. Suggestively, the earliest innovations of men resulted from accidents and from play, and man had only enough sophistication to retain what seemed best at the time. To introduce changes in living by actual design and with well-defined intent appears to have been unusual in the world of tribal peoples, and among ourselves it became important only following industrialization. Perfect creations may only be originated by perfect man or infallible deities; to date, neither are known to exist. Thus mortal men create new things, but rarely if ever do their inventions function as universally beneficial.

With this view of the inevitable obstacles brought about by technological changes I view the dehumanized and unnatural city setting as normal and even as expectable. I note also that urbanites are increasingly articulate in expressing concern about their environment. At the same time, the persons most responsible for the continuation or change of maladaptive conditions seem able to proceed as usual after making only token responses to public outcries. The remedial changes sponsored by various levels of government, civic groups, and industry will offer little in terms of meaningful, long-range relief. Perhaps we are awaiting a messiah to lead us out of our smoggy wilderness; what is more likely is that we will do little to change the city setting until one day the multiple ills strangle a major city. Something on the order of the New York area power failure in 1965, only much more fatal, may be needed to effect change. The sudden death of ten thousand persons from breathing lethal industrial air probably would awaken the national conscience and lead people to search seriously for answers. These answers even now seem to be just around the corner of known technology, but because they contradict our views of materialistic progress they remain only in the dreams of idealists.

Along the crowded streets of great cities we jostle persons who are faceless replicas of ourselves. When we range beyond the narrow confines of our job, neighborhood, and habitual haunts, we seldom look for or see anyone whom we know. The search for oneself in a city is lonely, but this is the way of the city. As the last earthly frontier, the city attracts loners, and for them its ways are congenial. Such persons sever ties with the past and often with the land, to search for greater and more satisfying achievement solely by their own endeavors. Personifying the pioneer type, such an individualist strikes off alone or with his family in search of a way of life considered as better. Among all our cities, possibly Los Angeles more than anywhere else presents individuals with the opportunities to find their own "thing," although it may or may not be termed as such. This most often results from the effort to find oneself through breaking molds of familiar patterns, a method most successful within the city's individualistic environment.

It is a paradox that we continue to attain almost fantastic levels of cultural complexity and specialization, while at the same time we negate fundamental bonds of social life, those within the nuclear family. In our almost fervent desire to come to grips effectively with almost every aspect of living, we strive to reduce all experience to the level of a tangible specific. At present we are quite capable of treating people as things; for instance, a waitress in a restaurant or a clerk in a store is more often considered as a thing rather than as a person. We also fully accept being treated as things. If you think this is not so, you should note the way in which you are regarded the next time you take your car to a garage for repairs or observe the manner in which you are dealt with on your next visit to a medical doctor or dentist. An even better example of the not-really-but-really-a-thing treatment is that which you receive from an airline "hostess." These behaviors reflect Thingness above all else. Thingness already has been extended to most nonrelatives and to distant relatives; it is now very close to the houses in which we dwell. We are approaching the point at which father is not "something" but "some thing," and mother is yet another "thing." Is all of this bad? Most emphatically, "NO." *It is the greatest individually liberating force ever achieved by man.* Because it is another of his great accidental achievements, however, it has inherent negative aspects which must be dealt with effectively. Perhaps herein lies the real challenge to anthropology, not to study traditional cultures, but to actively seek ways in which to develop a world of compatible individualists.

BIBLIOGRAPHY

CHAPTER 1

Patterns and Behavior

Benedict, Ruth, 1934, *Patterns of Culture.* Boston: Houghton Mifflin.
Kroeber, Alfred L., 1948, *Anthropology.* New York: Harcourt.

A Pattern Element: American Buttons

Olsen, Stanley J., 1963, "Dating Early Plain Buttons by Their Form," *Amer. Antiq.,* 28:551–554.

A Particular Pattern: Santa Claus

Barnett, James H., 1954, *The American Christmas.* New York: Macmillan.
Bode, Carl, 1959, *The Anatomy of American Popular Culture, 1840–1861.* Berkeley: University of California Press.
Paine, Albert B., 1904, *Th. Nast, His Period and His Pictures.* New York: Harper & Row.
Patterson, Samuel W., 1956, *The Poet of Christmas Eve: A Life of Clement Clarke Moore, 1779–1863.* New York: Morehouse-Gorham.
Sereno, Renzo, 1951, "Some Observations on the Santa Claus Custom," *Psychiat.,* 14:387–396.
Vail, R. W. G., 1951, "Santa Claus Visits the Hudson," *The New-York Hist. Soc. Quart. Bull.,* 35:337–343.

Wall, Alexander J., 1941, "St. Nicholas at the Society," *The New-York Hist. Soc. Quart. Bull.*, 25:10–16.
Wolf, Eric R., 1964, "Santa Claus: Notes on a Collective Representation," *Process and Pattern in Culture*, R. A. Manners, ed. Chicago: Aldine.

A Systemic Pattern: Treatment of Illness

Young, James H., 1961, *The Toadstool Millionaires: A Social History of Patent Medicines in America before Federal Regulation*. Princeton, N.J.: Princeton University Press.

Patterns and Evolution

Cohen, Ronald, 1962, "The Strategy of Social Evolution," *Anthropologica*, NS, 4:321–348.
Newsweek, March 11, 1968, p. 78.
Sahlins, Marshall D., and Elman R. Service, 1960, *Evolution and Culture*. Ann Arbor, Mich.: University of Michigan Press.

Culture and Society as Concepts

Kroeber, Alfred L., and Clyde Kluckhohn, 1963, *Culture: A Critical Review of Concepts and Definitions*. New York: Random House (Vintage Books).

Biases and Borrowings

Bradfield, Nancy, 1958, *Historical Costumes of England from the Eleventh to the Twentieth Century*. London: Harrap.
Burris-Meyer, Elizabeth, 1943, *This is Fashion*. New York: Harper & Row.
Crawford, Morris D. C., and Elizabeth G. Crawford, 1952, *The History of Lingerie in Pictures*. New York: Fairchild.
Cunnington, Cecil W., and Phillis Cunnington, 1951, *The History of Underclothes*. London: Michael Joseph.
Grass, Milton N., 1955, *History of Hosiery, from the Piloi of Ancient Greece to the Nylons of Modern America*. New York: Fairchild.
Laver, James, 1945, *Taste and Fashion, from the French Revolution to the Present Day*. London: Harrap.
Norris, Herbert, 1933, *Costume and Fashion, the Nineteenth Century*. Vol. 6. London: Dent.
Rhead, George W., 1906, *Chats on Costume*. London: T. Fisher Unwin.
Watson, Lillian Eichler, 1924, *The Customs of Mankind, with Notes on Modern Etiquette and the Newest Trend in Entertainment*. Garden City, N.Y.: Doubleday.
Wilcox, Ruth T., 1942, *The Mode in Costume*. New York: Scribner.
———, 1963, *Five Centuries of American Costume*. New York: Scribner.
Young, Agnes B., 1937, *Recurring Cycles of Fashion, 1760–1937*. New York: Harper & Row.

CHAPTER 2

Qualities of Time

Leach, E. R., 1954, "Primitive Time-Reckoning," *A History of Technology,* Vol. I, Charles Singer, and others, eds. New York: Oxford University Press, pp. 110–127.

Saulteaux Indian Time

Hallowell, A. I., 1937, "Temporal Orientation in Western Civilization and in a Pre-literate Society," *Amer. Anth.,* NS, 39:647–670.

Measuring Our Time

Britten, Frederick, 1956, *Old Clocks and Watches and their Makers: A Historical and Descriptive Account of the Different Styles of Clocks and Watches of the Past in England and Abroad Containing a List of Nearly 14,000 Makers,* Granville H. Baillie, and others, eds. London: E. & F. N. Spon.

Crombie, Alistair C., 1959, *Medieval and Early Modern Science,* 2 vol. Garden City, N.Y.: Doubleday.

Leach, E. R., *see* above under *Qualities of Time.*

Neugebauer, O., 1954, "Ancient Mathematics and Astronomy," *A History of Technology,* Vol. 1, Charles Singer, and others, eds. New York: Oxford University Press, pp. 785–803.

The Time of the Past

Gillispie, Charles C., 1959, *Genesis and Geology.* New York: Harper & Row.

Smith, Homer W., 1953, *Man and His Gods.* Boston: Little, Brown.

Yurok Indian Spatial Concepts

Waterman, Thomas T., 1920, "Yurok Geography," *Univ. of California Publ. in Amer. Arch. and Ethnol.,* 16:177–314.

Symbolizing Earthly Space

Bagrow, Leo, 1964, *History of Cartography,* rev. by R. A. Skelton. Cambridge, Mass.: Harvard University Press.

Discovering New Peoples

Bridges, Esteban Lucas, 1948, *Uttermost Part of the Earth.* London: Hodder.

Darwin, Charles, 1962, *The Voyage of the Beagle,* Leonard Engel, ed. Garden City, N.Y.: Doubleday.

Fitzroy, Robert, ed., 1839, *Narrative of the Surveying Voyages of His Majesty's*

Ships 'Adventure' and 'Beagle,' between the Years 1826 and 1836, Describing their Examination of the Southern Shores of South America, and the 'Beagle's' Circumnavigation of the Globe. Vol. 2, Proceedings of the Second Expedition, 1831–1836, under the Command of Captain Robert Fitz-Roy. London: Colburn.

Himmelfarb, Gertrude, 1962, Darwin and the Darwinian Revolution. Garden City, N.Y.: Doubleday.

CHAPTER 3

The African Adam

Darwin, Charles, 1898, The Descent of Man and Selection in Relation to Sex. New York: Appleton.

Hoebel, Edward A., 1966, Anthropology: the Study of Man. New York: Mc-Graw-Hill.

"The Origin of Man," Current Anthro., 1965, 6:342–431.

Ladders, Chains, and Links

Toulmin, Stephen, and June Goodfield, 1966, The Discovery of Time. New York: Harper & Row.

Modern Man

Howells, William W., 1966, "Homo Erectus," Sci. Amer., 215:46–53.

Species and Races

Dobzhansky, Theodosius, 1966, Heredity and the Nature of Man. New York: New American Library.

Montagu, Ashley, 1963, Anthropology and Human Nature. New York: Mc-Graw-Hill.

Human Races: A General Statement

Harris, Marvin, 1968, The Rise of Anthropological Theory. New York: Crowell.

"Statement on the Nature of Race and Race Differences," May 26, 1952, United Nations Educational, Scientific and Cultural Organization (reprinted in Current Anthro., 1961, 2:304–306).

CHAPTER 4

Lancaster, Jane B., 1968, "On the Evolution of Tool-Using Behavior," Amer. Anth., NS, 70:56–66.

The First Men

Clark, J. Desmond, 1963, "The Evolution of Culture in Africa," *Amer. Natural.*, 97:5–28.
Dart, Raymond A., 1949, "The Predatory Implemental Technique of Australopithecus," *Amer. Journ. of Phys. Anth.*, NS, 7:1–16.
———, 1960, "The Bone Tool-Manufacturing Ability of Australopithecus Prometheus," *Amer. Anth.*, NS, 62:134–143.
Leakey, L. S. B., 1951, *Olduvai Gorge*. London: Cambridge University Press.
Washburn, Sherwood L., 1960, "Tools and Human Evolution," *Sci. Amer.*, 203:63–75.

Fire and Man

Oakley, Kenneth P., 1961, "On Man's Use of Fire, with Comments on Toolmaking and Hunting," in "Social Life of Early Man," *Viking Fund Publ. in Anth.*, Sherwood L. Washburn, ed., 31:176–193.
Pfeiffer, John, Dec. 11, 1966, "When Homo Erectus Tamed Fire, He Tamed Himself," *The New York Times Magazine*, pp. 58–72.

Family Life Begins

Chance, M. R. A., 1962, "Social Behaviour and Primate Evolution," *Culture and the Evolution of Man*, Ashley Montagu, ed. New York: Oxford University Press, pp. 84–130.
DeVore, Irven, 1964, "The Evolution of Social Life," *Horizons of Anthropology*, Sol Tax, ed. Chicago: Aldine, pp. 25–35.
———, ed., 1965, *Primate Behavior*. New York: Holt, Rinehart and Winston, Inc.
Jay, Phyllis C., ed., 1968, *Primates*. New York: Holt, Rinehart and Winston, Inc.
Sahlins, Marshall D., 1960, "The Origin of Society," *Sci. Amer.*, 203:76–87.
Slater, Mariam K., 1959, "Ecological Factors in the Origin of Incest," *Amer. Anth.*, NS, 61:1042–1059.
Washburn, Sherwood L., and Phyllis C. Jay, eds., 1968, *Perspectives on Human Evolution*. New York: Holt, Rinehart, and Winston, Inc.

Language

Ervin, Susan M., 1964, "Language and Thought," *Horizons of Anthropology*, Sol Tax, ed. Chicago: Aldine, pp. 81–91.
Hockett, Charles F., 1960, "The Origin of Speech," *Sci. Amer.*, 203:88–96.
Reynolds, Peter C., 1968, "Evolution of Primate Vocal-Auditory Communication Systems," *Amer. Anth.*, NS, 70:300–308.

Technology

Binford, Lewis R., and Sally R. Binford, 1966, "A Preliminary Analysis of Functional Variability in the Mousterian of Levallois Facies," *Amer. Anth.*, NS, 68:238–295.

CHAPTER 5

Drives

Murdock, George P., 1945, "The Common Denominator of Cultures," *The Science of Man in the World Crisis*, Ralph Linton, ed. New York: Columbia University Press, pp. 123–142.

From Anxiety to Aggression

Leighton, Alexander H., 1949, *Human Relations in a Changing World*. New York: Dutton.

Aggression and Tribal Peoples

Chagnon, Napoleon A., 1968, *Yąnomamö, The Fierce People*. New York: Holt, Rinehart and Winston.
Radcliffe-Brown, Alfred R., 1922, *The Andaman Islanders*. Cambridge: Cambridge University Press.
"War: The Anthropology of Armed Conflict and Aggression," Dec. 1967, *Natural History*, pp. 39–70.

Ultimate Violence and Ourselves

Leighton, Alexander H., *see* above under *From Anxiety to Aggression*.

CHAPTER 6

Linton, Ralph, 1959, "The Natural History of the Family," *The Family: Its Function and Destiny*, Ruth N. Anshen, ed. New York: Harper & Row, pp. 30–52.
Murdock, George P., 1949, *Social Structure*. New York: Macmillan.

A Soviet Experiment

Geiger, Kent, 1956, "Changing Political Attitudes in Totalitarian Society," *World Politics*, 8:187–205.
Timasheff, Nicholas S., 1946, *The Great Retreat*. New York: Dutton.

The Nayar Novelty

Gough, E. Kathleen, 1959, "The Nayars and the Definition of Marriage," *The Journal of the Royal Anthropological Institute*, 89:23–34.

Dyads and Dads

Adams, Richard N., 1960, "An Inquiry into the Nature of the Family," *Essays in the Science of Culture,* Gertrude E. Dole and Robert L. Carneiro, eds. New York: Thomas Crowell, pp. 30–49.

Bureau of Census, 1963, "Families," *United States Census of Population, 1960.* Washington, D.C.: U. S. Dept. of Commerce, Bur. of Census.

Smith, Raymond T., 1956, *The Negro Family in British Guiana.* London: Routledge.

Mothers and Children

Minturn, Leigh, and William W. Lambert, 1964, *Mothers of Six Cultures.* New York: Wiley.

Whiting, Beatrice B., ed., 1963, *Six Cultures.* New York: Wiley.

Family Life in the United States

Linton, Ralph, *see* above under *Chapter 6.*

Murdock, George P., 1950, "Family Stability in Non-European Cultures," *Annals of the American Academy of Political and Social Science,* 272:195–201.

CHAPTER 7

Social Norms

Lowie, Robert H., 1948, *Social Organization.* New York: Holt, Rinehart and Winston, Inc.

Murdock, George P., 1949, *Social Structure.* New York: Macmillan.

Schusky, Ernest L., 1965, *Manual for Kinship Analysis.* New York: Holt, Rinehart and Winston, Inc.

Our Kinship Terms

Codere, Helen, 1955, "A Genealogical Study of Kinship in the United States," *Psychiatry,* 18:65–79.

Goodenough, Ward H., 1965, "Yankee Kinship Terminology: A Problem in Componential Analysis," *Amer. Anth.,* NS, 67:259–287.

Schneider, David M., 1968, *American Kinship.* Englewood Cliffs, N.J.: Prentice-Hall.

————, and George C. Homans, 1955, "Kinship Terminology and the American Kinship System," *Amer. Anth.,* NS, 57:1194–1208.

CHAPTER 8

The First Farmers

Braidwood, Robert J., 1960, "The Agricultural Revolution," *Sci. Amer.*, 203, No. 3:130–148.

———, and Bruce Howe, 1962, "Southwestern Asia Beyond the Lands of the Mediterranean Littoral," Courses Toward Urban Life, Robert Braidwood and Gordon Willey, eds., *Viking Fund Publ. in Anthropology*, 32:132–146.

The First Cities

Adams, Robert M., 1960, "The Origin of Cities," *Sci. Amer.*, 203, No. 3:153–168.

———, 1962, "Agriculture and Urban Life in Early Southwestern Iran," *Science*, 136:109–122.

Redfield, Robert, 1947, "The Folk Society," *Amer. Jour. of Sociology*, 52: 293–308.

Types of Cities

Redfield, Robert, and Milton B. Singer, 1954, "The Cultural Role of Cities," *Economic Development and Cultural Change*, 3:53–73.

Timbuctoo

Miner, Horace, 1953, *The Primitive City of Timbuctoo*. Princeton, N.J.: Princeton University Press.

Los Angeles

Caughey, John W., 1940, *California*. New York: Prentice-Hall.

Dumke, Glenn S., 1944, *The Boom of the Eighties*. San Marino, Calif.: Huntington Library.

Los Angeles: 1900–1961, 1962, Los Angeles: Los Angeles County Museum.

Winther, Oscar O., 1947, "The Rise of Metropolitan Los Angeles," *The Huntington Library Quarterly*, 10:391–405.

CHAPTER 9

Herber, Lewis, 1965, *Crisis in Our Cities*. Englewood Cliffs, N.J.: Prentice-Hall.

INDEX